THE
OUTDOOR ROOM

THE
OUTDOOR ROOM

GARDEN DESIGN FOR LIVING

DAVID STEVENS

Principal photography by
JERRY HARPUR

RANDOM HOUSE
New York

To Pauline, my wife,
without whom none of this would have been possible

Originally published in Great Britain by
Frances Lincoln Limited, London.

Library of Congress Cataloging in Publication
data is available.
ISBN 0-679-43467-4

Printed in Italy by New Interlitho Italia S.p.A.
9 8 7 6 5 4 3 2 1
First U.S. Edition

Half title page An irresistible
invitation to step into the outdoor
room, designer Mirabel Osler.

Frontispiece A breakfast deck
catches the early morning sunshine,
designer Christopher Masson.

Contents page, left to right
A wrought iron seat with a marine
flavor, designer Malcolm Hillier.
A white gate in a kitchen garden,
designer Edwina von Gal.
A pot planted by Elspeth Merton.
A circular brick terrace, designer
Michael Balston.

CONTENTS

THE OUTDOOR ROOM

Over the past few years garden design has become increasingly popular. Whether this explosion of interest is a fashionable trend or a worthwhile development in a genuine artform remains to be seen. In either case, as a practicing designer I welcome it, because it indicates an increased awareness – among amateurs as well as professionals – that the area around our homes is a valuable one, which can greatly extend the potential of our living space, and our enjoyment of it.

A successful garden design gets the best out of what is essentially an outdoor room, making it look good and reflect individual needs and a contemporary lifestyle. Often, though, the end result is a mishmash of ideas and planting that does little to serve the owner and makes maintenance a nightmare. A preoccupation with the past – evident in certain parts of the world – may mean that any discernible style is likely to be broadly classified as "cottage garden" or "formal," the latter embracing a fondness for parterres and sheared hedging.

The truth of the matter is that garden design *is* an artform, yet the way in which many garden designers, landscape architects, and environmental professionals are trained often leaves much to be desired.

Instead of a broad education where associated trades, and I call them that intentionally, are taught to interrelate, students are pigeonholed into increasingly specialized fields. The results of this may become obvious when, say, an interior designer or a conventionally trained architect attempts to design a garden: all the skills, the understanding of spatial relationships, and the sheer down-to-earth commonsense applied to the design of the interior seem to evaporate when transported outside.

Of course there are, and always have been, gifted designers who could tackle the whole spectrum of art and architecture. Many have practiced as architects and names such as Edwin Lutyens, Norman Shaw, Charles Rennie Mackintosh, and Frank Lloyd Wright are synonymous with the ability to create a totally integrated environment, both inside and outside the home. Lutyens, one of the greatest British garden designers, used a brilliantly vernacular style that extends the lines of his superb buildings into the landscape. Though Gertrude Jekyll certainly breathed life into Lutyens' geometry, it was his feeling for form and space that provided the framework in which her planting could be seen at its best.

For an understanding of the true relationship between architecture and landscape, one need look no further than Frank Lloyd Wright's famous house Fallingwater, in Pennsylvania. Built over a waterfall, the structure is an integral, organic part of its setting. The same organic approach is evident in the horizontal lines of his Prairie Style houses, and his Taliesin West in Arizona, a building which presents a breathtaking unity with its wonderful desert site.

Both Wright and Lutyens also fashioned everything inside the houses they designed: this is the essence of *total* design. Some might argue that this has little to do with domestic gardens, but my point is that in order to design one area properly you have to have an excellent understanding of the others. The only design school to address this issue was the German Bauhaus, founded in 1919 by Walter Gropius. Within its campus was born the Modern Movement, the most influential movement in art, architecture, and design of the twentieth century. The broad curriculum at the Bauhaus included theater, metalwork, architecture, and art: most important, students were obliged to master at least one craft skill. In the fourteen-year period of its existence – until it was dissolved by Hitler – the Bauhaus unlocked an entirely new way of thinking about design that turned its back on the tired old Beaux Arts school.

The ideas and the ideals of the Bauhaus, moreover, were not crushed, despite its demise in Germany. Walter Gropius, Mies van der Rohe, Marcel Breuer, Josef

Opposite and below A close relationship between house and garden is achieved at Folly Farm in Berkshire, England. It is a fine example of the collaborative genius of architect Edwin Lutyens and plantswoman Gertrude Jekyll. The mellow tones and textures of the brick-built house are picked up in the brick paths and low walls that both link and divide a complex arrangement of "outdoor rooms." The more complicated Lutyens' patterns, the simpler Miss Jekyll's planting became.

Albers, and László Moholy-Nagy, all of whom had been masters at the school,
headed for America where they were welcomed with open arms. Gropius became
Head of Architecture at Harvard and Mies, Dean at Chicago. In this free-thinking
country, with its melting pot of new immigrants and new ideas, unfettered by the
exigencies of a stultifying tradition, the Modern Movement flourished. Despite
the fact that the initial focus was on architecture, a greater awareness of landscape
and landscape architecture also came into being. A new style of American garden
design gradually emerged, which rejected the old formal styles, relics of a
European past.

Such changes, of course, do not happen overnight. It is difficult to discard one
tradition and immediately replace it with another. Although the ideas of the
Modern Movement were now being taught and accepted in America, the way in
which they were interpreted was still experimental and initially the apparent
explosion of freedom brought with it an element of chaos and lack of real purpose.
But freedom also breeds enthusiasm and confidence.

The pioneers of the revolution were Thomas Church, Garrett Eckbo, and,

slightly later, Lawrence Halprin. All three trained as landscape architects; all three broke radical new ground in the design process and created the basis of the new American garden. The space around the house was now seen as an extension of the rooms inside the building and the links between inside and outside were emphasized in line and materials. Form followed function, and the gardens came not only to reflect the house they adjoined and the landscape in which they were set, but also the personality of the owner.

In England, World War II ensured that the Modern Movement got off to a slow start and, compared with the developments taking place in America, its influence on gardens was initially minimal. Only Christopher Tunnard, a gifted young Canadian, embraced the philosophy and created a small number of innovative compositions. His book *Gardens in the Modern Landscape* is a classic and well worth getting if you can find a copy, since, sadly, it is out of print. It was illustrated by Gordon Cullen, a talented artist and townscape consultant who produced beautiful and perceptive studies of many English county towns in the nineteen sixties and seventies. Such work is of enormous benefit to any aspiring

Above Geometry was the mainstay of much of the early work undertaken by the new wave of American garden designers, as is evident in this composition by Garrett Eckbo.

Here, pattern is all important, with triangles inserted into the rectangular pool, which is surrounded by angular raised beds and a high perimeter wall.

The circular bowls of the water feature act as a counterpoint, adding both sound and movement, while planting softens the boundary and contains the space.

Opposite In the vanguard of contemporary American garden design, Wolfgang Oehme and James van Sweden, building on the foundation of the Modern Movement, unite architecture, site, and planting in their dynamic designs. White picket fencing, in keeping with the house, contains this small paved sitting area.

Below A strong architectural pattern is overlaid with planting which, by disguising the boundaries, enhances the feeling of space in this outdoor dining area designed by contemporary German architect Richard Bödeker.

garden designer, since it opens the eyes to the way in which the urban scene is put together.

Today we are several decades into Modernism and, while its thesis still holds good, the way in which it can be interpreted has inevitably, and naturally, shifted. Gardens and lifestyles have changed, the first on average becoming smaller, the second, a good deal faster. With this change, the concept of the garden as an outdoor room, closely related in form and function to the rooms inside, has become stronger. Both rooms and gardens have floors, walls, furnishings, ornaments, lighting, and different themes. Gardens, too, have ceilings, in the shape of tree canopies, pergolas, or overheads. Plants and other features can all move from outside to in: why should the traffic be one way only? There need be no real division between inside and out, so why *do* we have such hangups in exterior planning?

This is the crux of the matter. Most of us are simply not conditioned to think of manipulating or designing the space outside, although the principles are the same as those that apply inside the house. Garden design is no more a mystery than interior design; in fact they are remarkably similar and incredibly easy to grasp. Above all else, the creation of a garden is immensely satisfying. This is one of the few spaces over which you have complete control: so don't waste it! Use it and enjoy it!

PLANNING FOR LIVING OUTSIDE

Gardens, just as much as houses, are for living in. And the ideal garden is not only a beautiful place to be, it is tailormade to fit the needs of those who use it.

For some, the garden is an all-absorbing passion. They are never happier than when out digging, planting, pruning – and enjoying the fruits of their labors, which may stimulate the palate as well as the eye.

For others, the garden is a place in which to be calm, to relax, to welcome and entertain visitors, to cook, to eat. If you are very young it is a place to play in, whether skipping games or hide-and-seek.

Creating a garden that suits your lifestyle and looks stylish while satisfying all your practical needs is a challenge . . . and a pleasure.

On the first fine day of spring there is a stirring in millions of homes, a natural awakening from winter that is as evident in people as it is in animals emerging after months of hibernation. And with this awakening there comes a renewed awareness of the space outside, a need to enjoy the garden, and, often, a strong urge to modify it or to add to the composition in some way. This is the outdoor equivalent of spring cleaning and redecorating indoors.

Almost inevitably there is a rush for the nearest garden center or nursery, a spree of random purchases and a dash to get them home as quickly as possible. The end result of this impetuous approach is, more often than not, haphazard, with pots, plants, and paving purchased and positioned on impulse. It is hardly surprising, then, that so many gardens amount to little more than an unrelated jumble of features and planting; they do not work properly either in practical or visual terms, and fail to serve you, the occupier, to best advantage.

Change and modification are, sometimes, both valid and necessary in making a well-ordered garden, but their effect on an unplanned space can be disastrous. Features and furnishings can be inappropriately placed and plants doomed to failure, because they have been chosen without regard to their suitability for the site. If the occupiers of such gardens worked out how much they had spent on them over a period of years, the total would probably be horrifying. If, on the other hand, the same calculations were made in relation to a space that had been sensibly and sensitively designed, the picture would be much rosier, and a lot of hard-earned cash, as well as unnecessary effort, would have been saved.

Planning is the key to success. By taking time in the planning process, beginning by checking out exactly what you have inside and outside your space, as well as inside the house itself, you can work out just what you want and begin to mold it into a working pattern that meets your own unique requirements. People often tend to think of house and garden as two quite separate elements: they should, in fact, be considered as a single entity, the one relating to and dependent on the other. Indeed, the ability to view the spaces that surround our homes as outdoor rooms is central to the evolution of a composition that reflects the personality and needs of the occupier. Environment, climate, and geographical location, as well as lifestyle, are all major factors influencing the final form these rooms will take.

THE LOCAL ENVIRONMENT

Wherever a garden is located, the surrounding environment should play a major role in the form and choice of hard materials that make up the space. Until comparatively recent times, there was a natural and inevitable respect for local materials and styles of building – inevitable because transporting different materials across country was either impossible or dauntingly costly, and local labor and skills tended to stay put and to build in a vernacular style. It is for this reason that long-

Previous pages Eating and entertaining take on a new pleasurable dimension out of doors. Here, there is ample room for sitting and dining, and the barbecue is sensibly sited undercover. An open fire alongside it can be enjoyed when evenings grow cooler. This space is attractively contained by an old, but productive, apple tree.

Opposite House and garden can, and should, be planned as a single entity. To link the white garden with the dining room of a Cape Dutch house in South Africa, the owner chose crisp bands of natural stone. The feeling of movement between inside and outside is heightened by the use of running bond and precise jointing that draws the eye outward.

White standard roses, stone ornaments on the brick step, and symmetrically planted beds focus the attention on the centrally placed white seat. When the rose hedge has grown a little, to mask the trellis pillars in the garden behind, the picture will be perfect.

established towns are so successful in visual terms.

You only have to walk down the main street of an old town to observe that the architecture is much of a kind; most of the houses, although perhaps built at different times and to different patterns, have an affinity with one another that arises from the use of common materials. If the area is rich in local stone, then that stone is used in the buildings; in other areas, brick or lumber cladding may predominate. Delight in attention to detail, such as fine old period railings, particular brick patterns, decorative tiled paths, and richly molded woodwork is evident. Consistency of approach to both house and surrounding structures is achieved through the use of the same or matching materials not only for those walls that run out from the building to enclose the garden, but also for internal garden walls and paving.

Today the vast choice of materials available often produces gardens that are driven by whim rather than regard for the surrounding environment, and the end result is, more often than not, awkward and uncomfortable. So look around you, at your street, at your neighborhood, analyze what you see and try to match themes and materials where you can. If you live in a stone house, then old stone flags and drystone walls will be in perfect harmony. If your house is brick, of whatever period, then think of using brick, sensibly teamed with another material, such as a neat precast concrete slab, in the garden. Local building styles and materials, wherever they are, will modify the architecture and hard landscape in a similar way. Brownstone buildings in New York or clapboard houses in the Midwest have their own richly vernacular style. Where buildings are concrete, then this too can be extended into the outside living space.

We shall be looking in more detail at how to use plants in Chapter 5, but for the moment we can note the obvious potential in choosing those that grow well locally. Again, observation of neighboring gardens may pay off: look around you and respect what you see. When assessing planting possibilities, do not forget the "borrowed" element of any plan: trees, shrubs, and plants growing in neighboring gardens, but visible from your own, can be drawn into your composition. This not only provides a greater feeling of continuity, in exactly the same way as using fabrics and color schemes in adjoining rooms inside the house, it also helps increase the apparent size of your own plot, particularly if you can disguise the boundary and let species run together.

Whether your garden is situated in city or country will obviously play an important role in the way you approach your design. Landform, too, is likely to influence your choice of both the hard and planted elements of your environment. Where slopes are involved, an urban approach might use crisp paving and terracing, while in the country rolling lawns and soft planting would be altogether more suitable.

Opposite and above Observing, and respecting, the character of the surrounding area and working whenever possible in the vernacular style, is an important first step in good garden design. In a small London garden (opposite) bricks, of the same gray as those used for neighboring buildings, link the outdoor rooms. The strong pattern around the pond draws the eye inward away from the boundary – a particularly useful strategy when the view beyond is less than beautiful.

In a California garden (above) a sun-bleached deck and a wooden pergola create a comfortable space for lounging, while warm-colored paving slabs pick up the roof color.

Opposite Plentiful rain encourages lush growth in temperate zones, where subtle colors are enhanced by soft light. Shade-loving ferns and ivies near the house lead on to a restrained color scheme in the sunnier part of this romantically disheveled-looking garden in southern England. Its appearance belies its careful planning.

Below The Mediterranean climate makes this Los Angeles garden perfect for outdoor living. As in the tropics, the brilliance of the light permits the use of strong vivid hues. Despite the lack of rain in summer, roses, with their long roots, flourish.
Designer Mel Light

WORKING WITH THE CLIMATE

This complex and variable subject can be broken down into two broad areas that are of prime interest to the garden user. The first is the general or regional climatic zone in which you live. This will have certain characteristics in common with other areas around the globe that are broadly described in the same way, whether cool temperate, Mediterranean, subtropical, or tropical. If you are new to a neighborhood, find out about the local "known quantities:" the direction of prevailing winds, average seasonal temperatures and annual rainfall, the average number of sunny days each year, the likely onset and duration of frost, and so on. While these are the regional norm, there are other more localized conditions described as "microclimates." A classic example is that of the west coast of Scotland, which is on a similar latitude to Moscow or parts of Hudson Bay. While the last two experience fiercely cold winters, the west coast of Scotland, warmed by the Gulf Stream, has extraordinarily mild weather throughout the year. A few miles inland the benefit of this warming oceanic current is lost and temperatures drop dramatically. Warmer microclimates occur, too, near large inland bodies of water as well as in cities, where heat is retained in the fabric of buildings that also provide shelter from wind.

On an even smaller scale, the ground beneath a sunny wall may enjoy particularly sheltered conditions, while the area beneath the overhanging eaves of a house may receive little or no rainfall, creating its own dry microclimate.

An unusually cold microclimate may occur at the bottom of a hill or depression surrounded by higher ground. This is known as a frost hollow and comes about when cold air, which is heavy, drains down a slope and gathers at the bottom from where it is unable to escape. The temperature in the hollow drops to below that of the surrounding higher ground, and frost occurs. Gardens in such positions will experience particularly severe conditions. The same effect may be apparent half-way down a hill where a wall or thick hedge can trap cold air and stop it "draining" away. The answer may be to open a gap in the hedge or to create a "moongate" in the wall so that the air can continue on its way.

As a general rule, work with climate rather than against it, accepting local conditions for what they are and planting your garden accordingly. Coastal gardeners may have to limit their repertoire to plants that tolerate salt, and take special measures, perhaps by planting high hedges or digging sunken gardens, to provide shelter from gusty winds. Gardeners in regions where summers are likely to be dry and water resources limited – this applies particularly to Mediterranean regions – should opt for plants that are known to be drought-tolerant. In cool, upland areas, where rock may outcrop frequently, tough, hardy subjects are the order of the day; there is little point in planting tender specimens. Again, it pays to observe which plants flourish in your part of the world.

PERSONALITY AND LIFESTYLE

Of all the factors that make one garden different from another, personality is the most significant. If you have a dozen plots side by side, with the same shape, size, aspect, slope, soil (and any number of other common factors), they are all likely to look very different. The same, of course, applies to houses, and on an estate with a hundred similar façades each internal space will have its own style and character. While the outward, visible stamp of individuality is obviously very important in a garden, it remains little more than a "stamp" if the space itself has not been planned with a view to what you and your family like and need, now and in the future.

If you employ a professional garden designer their prime job is to analyze exactly what you want and to mold it into a pattern that is just right for you. He or she will get a feeling for your personality, your likes and dislikes, discuss the budget, look at your lifestyle, talk to the kids, make a fuss of the pets, and make a note of the colors you like and the way you have treated the rooms inside the house. Only when they have elicited all this information can they confidently embark on creating a garden that fits you like a glove.

This is the process that *you* need to go through if you are going to design the outdoor room or rooms yourself. Analyze yourself, your family, look at all these things and make a checklist of what you want. Take your time, forget the impulse buys and start to work out what you really need rather than what you think might look pretty. The garden is a working space that can provide beauty and function in equal quantities. Good design is not about ostentation and overcomplication: it is about simplicity, fitness for purpose, and personality. If you can remember this alone, your garden is on the way to being a success.

Functions of outdoor rooms

While most people are familiar with the *idea* of gardens as outdoor rooms, most have real difficulty in putting that idea into practice. There seems to be some kind of psychological barrier that, while allowing us to effectively plan the rooms inside the house, prevents us from thinking about the rooms outside in the same way. In fact, when thinking about them generally in terms of function, layout, and decoration, there is little difference between the two. Rooms both inside and out can serve specific purposes; corridors and paths provide links and access; color schemes need to be thought about and implemented; plants, albeit different species, flourish on both sides of the walls and windows; furnishings, ornaments, and incidental features add finishing touches to both spheres. The principal hurdle to overcome is thinking of house and garden as two separate elements. We should be considering a total environment that includes *everything* inside the boundaries: backyard, front lawn, and the house. The major significant difference is that the garden is a living, changing entity, while the house is not.

Above Plan, if you can, a quiet corner of the garden just for dreaming.

Below This is an ideal outdoor room with lots of potential uses. Pretty and secluded, it is an inviting place to have breakfast or a coffee break, to sit and read or write, to pursue a gentle pastime, such as painting, sewing, or yoga, to enjoy an early evening cocktail or dine with friends.
Designer Christopher Masson

We have already looked at ways of linking the house and garden visually by the use of hard materials, but an equally strong bond is created by establishing links of identity. This is the crux of the matter, and for outdoor rooms to be satisfactory, they need an identity that can be reinforced by the way in which each is furnished.

The heart of any living space, inside or out, is the area where the greatest number of activities take place. In a garden this is the terrace or patio that usually, but not always, adjoins the rear of the house. Clearly, if sun is important to you, and the area just to the rear of the house is in shade for much of the day, then the patio may need to be situated elsewhere. In this case, it can be linked back to the house by a path or paving.

The terrace will be your major living space for sitting, dining, entertaining, children's play, barbecuing, household chores (such as ironing, which is a great deal more pleasurable to do outside), and a hundred other activities, from dismantling motorcycles to preparing hanging baskets or bathing the dog. It will, in fact, be the hub of the garden. If the terrace adjoins the house, it can be linked not only physically but also visually with the building, making the transition between inside and out a natural one and, in kind climates, virtually imperceptible. Its treatment, then, is likely to be more formal, more "architectural" than that of other, more distant, areas of the garden.

Outdoor rooms, like the rooms inside the house, may be designed to serve one predominant function. Thus, if space is available, you may plan a rumpus room for children – planted with practicality in mind and partly paved, perhaps, for bicycle

riding, with a sandbox, swing, climbing frame, and so on – within sight of the house. A keen gardener and cook might want to set aside room near the house for a kitchen garden, which, with the many ornamental varieties of vegetable available today, could be as beautiful as it is productive. The farthest reaches of the plot offer the possibility of a retreat, a secret leafy sanctuary with a hammock for adults or a treehouse for older children. In a large garden this area might contain fruit trees and areas of rougher grass naturalized with bulbs and wild flowers, a haven for wildlife.

While those who are interested in maintaining (or attaining!) physical fitness can work out perfectly well in the smallest of yards or on the tiniest terrace, you may wish to incorporate games "rooms" – fitness center, croquet lawn, tennis court, swimming pool – into your garden plan if you have the space. These, too, will need subtle and successful integration with adjoining areas.

Less glamorous, but essential "utility" items, such as a shed, compost heap, incinerator, and, in country areas, septic tank need sensible siting, probably some distance from the house; closer to it, provision must be made for clotheslines, garbage disposal, and, possibly, an oil storage tank.

Once all needs have been met, the style in which they are clothed inevitably reflects your personal preferences and way of living: this may mean much paving and minimal maintenance; it may mean a softer, more fluid, and fragrant composition (indicative of a more leisurely, romantic approach) or a wild, back-to-nature "ecological" state of apparent abandon. All are fine – though the last, incidentally, often produces a considerably more unruly and work-intensive room than might be expected!

Below Some areas of the garden, like rooms inside the house, are clearly devoted to one main function. Swimming and related pleasures – sunbathing and sipping poolside drinks – are the principal activities in this sheltered, secluded spot, sited conveniently close to the house. The curves of the pool are cleverly offset to incorporate the steps, while the surrounding paving, tonally in harmony with the cottage roof, provides a low-key background.

THE CHANGING GARDEN

In addition to finding out what you want and enjoy now, it makes sense to take into account how you envisage your garden space developing along with your changing lifestyle and needs over a period of years. This is the principle which lies behind my changing garden design. It allows you to budget sensibly and to add to or modify the area without necessarily changing the underlying framework.

The demands on the garden space change: family life brings a wide range of boisterous activities that rarely sit comfortably with delicate planting. As time passes, the pressure on a garden may become less while the time available to tend it increases – though in later years the most practical way to garden may be with raised beds. And if demands change, so, too, do budgets: if space for a swimming pool is allocated at the planning stage, though this may be some years before you can actually afford one, its eventual integration into the garden design will be straightforward.

A three-stage design like the one shown here for a small backyard could take a family all the way through their life together. Though, in practice, this may seldom happen, you can plan to adapt the space over as long a period as is necessary. The principle can be applied to any area and is very flexible.

Stage 1: Basic design for single person/young couple

The starting point is a low-cost, easy maintenance framework. It can be adapted and different features added to suit changing needs. The main floor surface is gravel, which makes a pleasing contrast with the small paved dining area; planting is attractive but undemanding, and screens and fences are all built from secondhand or recycled lumber.

The plot is small: 30ft/9m long by 20ft/6m wide. Setting the design at an angle to the boundaries maximizes the available and visual space.

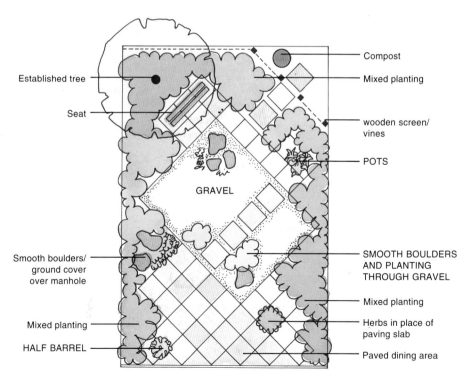

Established tree

Seat

Compost

Mixed planting

wooden screen/vines

POTS

GRAVEL

Smooth boulders/ground cover over manhole

SMOOTH BOULDERS AND PLANTING THROUGH GRAVEL

Mixed planting

Mixed planting

Herbs in place of paving slab

HALF BARREL

Paved dining area

Stage 2: The garden for young children

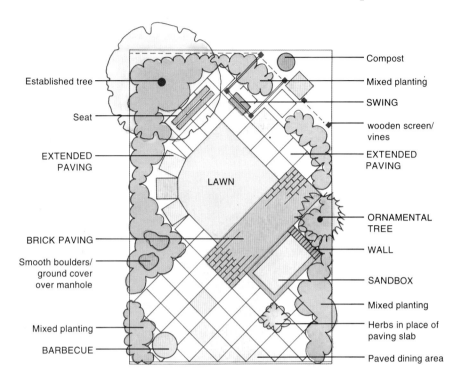

Established tree

Seat

EXTENDED PAVING

LAWN

BRICK PAVING

Smooth boulders/ ground cover over manhole

Mixed planting

BARBECUE

Compost

Mixed planting

SWING

wooden screen/ vines

EXTENDED PAVING

ORNAMENTAL TREE

WALL

SANDBOX

Mixed planting

Herbs in place of paving slab

Paved dining area

A couple with young children have different demands, though the budget is probably still limited. Lawn has replaced the gravel as a play surface; there is a raised sandbox near the house and a swing at the end of the garden. Bricks make a good surface for tricycle riding as well as introducing an interesting change of pace, pattern, color, and texture. The cost of these and the paving extension around the lawn is relatively low.

Stage 3: The final garden

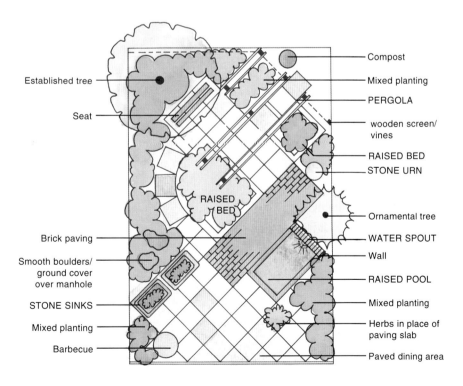

Established tree

Seat

Brick paving

Smooth boulders/ ground cover over manhole

STONE SINKS

Mixed planting

Barbecue

RAISED BED

Compost

Mixed planting

PERGOLA

wooden screen/ vines

RAISED BED

STONE URN

Ornamental tree

WATER SPOUT

Wall

RAISED POOL

Mixed planting

Herbs in place of paving slab

Paved dining area

This design could take a family through their life together – to retirement. Once the children have grown, the sandbox can safely be turned into a raised pool; an easy-to-tend raised bed replaces the lawn and acts as a pivot to the whole composition, in which a pergola spans the path to the seat.

ASSESSING YOUR SITE

If you are to design or redesign the space around your home so that it looks attractive, is practical, and serves you well, you need to find out everything about your garden. This involves not only checking its dimensions but obtaining and assimilating as much information as possible about its physical characteristics, both inside and beyond its boundaries.

Go out with a notepad, pencil, and measuring tape and make a simple survey, recording all your observations on a rough outline drawing of the site. This information will serve as the basis for an accurate scale drawing – an essential and invaluable tool, and the key to any successful design.

Previous pages A sloping site, nearby woodland, and established planting have influenced the layout of this garden.
Designers Wayne Winterrowd and Joe Eck

Opposite In Frank Cabot's garden in New York State, an established sugar maple (*Acer saccharum*) has been skillfully incorporated in an intimate sitting area.

When assessing your site, note the position of established trees first on your survey and then on your scale drawing. They will inevitably play a major role in your new design.

Below A sturdy seat built around the trunk of an established oak transforms a hitherto unused part of the garden into a pleasantly shaded retreat in the summer months.

When ordering fitted carpet, buying wallpaper, or a new drape fabric, it is customary, and essential, first to measure the floor, walls, and windows. No self-respecting interior designer would present you with a scheme for a new kitchen, which is likely to cost a small fortune, sketched out roughly on the back of an envelope. Yet some landscape contractors and many homeowners do just that for the garden, forging ahead without taking the first essential and simple step of checking its dimensions. The outcome, of course, is far from satisfactory, for in a garden as in a kitchen these dimensions are the basis for all that follows. They enable you to plan with certainty, to order accurate quantities of materials, and, if you need them, to obtain quotations from contractors.

Not everyone, of course, is designing from scratch. Most people do not embark on a wholesale redesigning of the garden as soon as they move into a new house. It is usually preferable to allow as much as a year to see which plants are worth saving (bulbs may not be apparent at first) and to eliminate weeds.

Assessing your outdoor space heightens your awareness of all the influences that come to bear on it. The assessment, which can be likened to building up a comprehensive picture of the site, is carried out in two stages. The first stage is a simple survey, which involves measuring the plot and gathering as much information as possible about its physical attributes, such as garden views, prevailing winds, location, and soil type. These dimensions and details are all entered on a simple outline plan. In the second stage, with the fact-finding completed, you are ready to produce a scale drawing of your present site, the essential basis for further planning.

VIEWS TO ENHANCE OR DISGUISE

Within any space, there are a multitude of possible views, dependent only on the number of viewpoints. Inside the house, views may be restricted by walls or opened up by doors and windows. Where walls are pierced by windows, there is an immediate visual link with the landscape outside, emphasizing once more the importance of considering house and garden as a complete unit.

When you measure up the house and garden for the survey, you note the position of all doors and windows. This is not simply to identify points of access, it is to establish exactly which views are available from which rooms, both up and downstairs. Everyone, no matter how keen they are on outside living, spends more time in the house than in the garden, and some rooms are used much more than others. High on the list are the kitchen and living rooms. Upstairs, there are usually bedrooms, though in some homes the living areas may be here, too. Do not categorize rooms according to whether or not you think the view is important. Our own bedroom has low-level windows, only 18in/450mm from the floor. From a standing position, the view is lost; but in the mornings we look out across open countryside to distant woods. I cannot imagine a more pleasant way to start the day and the view is infinitely variable, according to the season.

It may be the view from the bathroom that is stunning: capitalize on it, as on any beautiful view. I once had a battle with an interior designer who was insisting on using heavy baronial drapes in a bathroom – we were working on a castle – although they all but obscured the magnificent view across the moors outside. I finally managed to persuade him to frame the window with soft net drapes that encouraged the view out, and to link the interior color scheme with the colors of the landscape outside. Whether a superb landscape or a close-up of your neighbor's dilapidated shed, a fine group of shrubs or a neglected jungle, the view from inside to out is not to be ignored. Note on your survey all or any of these things. Once outside, views expand, ranging from the downright awful through the merely mundane to the sublime. Although the latter is certainly a possibility – a glimpse of a church across the fields or a dramatic seascape would both qualify – the first two categories are the ones most often encountered.

While fine views may need enhancing or framing in some way, their more mediocre counterparts may need screening. The latter can be done with planting or by installing more permanent structures, such as overhead beams, walls, or pergolas. Whatever materials or technique you use will depend on what views are available, and how they relate to the house and garden. This is where a camera will be useful. A photograph can often focus your attention better, allowing you to plan in a more specific way than a general view. It is amazing how much detail you start to see in a photograph, and the ability to focus both mind and eye is one of the designer's most valuable tools.

Below Magnificent views such as this are a rare and priceless asset. Capitalize on a good view by framing it and drawing it into the nearer composition. Here, beautifully detailed gates and simple white piers, reinforced by trees to either side, frame the spectacular slopes of Table Mountain in South Africa. Subtle pastels in the planting allow the eye to roam beyond the controlled environment of the garden into the wilder world beyond.

Neighboring sites

Most of us live in close proximity to other people, and whether neighbors get on well together or not, their lives inevitably impinge on one another's to some degree. There are, of course, neighbors who are such good friends that boundaries can be dispensed with altogether and their plots can run together. This doubles the available space at a stroke, but it also means that they both have to plan in a cooperative coherent way, which is not always easy. Such an arrangement most often arises when parents move into the house next door. If the synergy is right, this can be wonderful, with all the advantages of the extended family.

Of course, situations can and do change, and it is worth bearing in mind that boundaries may eventually have to be relocated, so plan the overall layout accordingly.

Sometimes neighbors pose problems. I once had some who went in for growing goutweed in a big way. This pernicious weed soon infected our garden and took months to eradicate. Though it originated next door, it was very much our problem. Overhanging trees, new garden buildings, and barbecues all fall into the same category: they can cause a nuisance, so take them into account when surveying your space.

Above The view from inside to out is one of the most important to the garden designer. Here the visual link is emphasized by the alignment of major features of interest – path, steps, walls, and beds – with the wide french windows.

Designer Jenny Robinson

LOCATION AND ITS IMPACT

One of the most important factors to take into account in any space, indoors and out, is the position of the sun as it moves overhead throughout the day. This largely determines not only how you use the garden but also how you plant it. If you are not certain of the orientation of your garden, use a magnetic compass to check it out, and note it on your survey.

The sun rises in the east and sets in the west, and it is a good idea to draw this on your plan by simply describing an arc that traces its course throughout the day. The height of the sun in the sky and the length of shadows it casts vary according to season and latitude. In the winter, the sun is much lower in the sky, and houses, sheds, trees, and hedges all cast longer shadows than they do in summer. It is worth noting the seasonal differences in length on your survey, so that you can see which parts of the garden enjoy sun at which time of day. It may mean, for example, that in summer much of a small garden or yard is in sun until late in the afternoon, while in winter it is in shade after midday.

The slope of a site has a considerable effect on its exposure. If a garden slopes toward the midday sun, the angle between it and the sun decreases and the area warms up more quickly in spring. This physical advantage makes the growing of crops a good deal easier; it may also be an ideal place to site solar panels for heating a swimming pool or water for the house. Conversely, a garden that slopes away from the midday sun is cold, since the effect of the sun is minimized and the ground is slow to warm up.

Opposite Try to organize your sitting areas so that you have a choice, as here, between sun and shade. A low, unobtrusive boxwood hedge and flowerbed define the limits of these two outdoor rooms while preserving a feeling of spaciousness. *Designer Andrew Pfeiffer*

Left Where you place a seat is largely determined by the garden's exposure – the way it faces. This beautifully crafted bench catches the afternoon sun. Flanked by matching Versailles tubs it makes an impressive focal point.

SHELTER AND SHADE

In temperate climates, lack of shelter often prevents people using the garden as much as they might like. There are many sunny days in autumn, winter, and spring when they would like to relax outside if it were not for a chill breeze. Both their use and enjoyment of the garden would be greatly increased by the simple provision of shelter.

When carrying out your survey, analyze the force and direction of the prevailing wind, and note if there are any areas in your garden that are naturally sheltered. Most will have such places, under trees or in the lee of a thick hedge; check them out on several occasions and under different conditions to get a realistic impression of the amount of shelter they afford.

If you need to erect some form of shelter, remember that a solid screen, such as a wall or fence, is not always a satisfactory answer, since a wind striking the face may be deflected up and over the barrier, creating a turbulent area on the other side. A better solution is a slatted fence or honeycomb-brick wall, which filters the wind rather than stopping it dead. Both of these structures benefit from planting, which can be used as a windbreak in its own right.

In hot climates, shelter is needed from the sun rather than wind, and here overhead structures, pergolas, awnings, umbrellas, and blinds come into their own, while tree canopies cast dappled shade, providing a soft, natural ceiling.

Above A small leafy bower high above the streets of New York needs shelter from high winds and hot sun. Planting provides an attractive and efficient wind filter, as well as affording privacy. A thin awning reduces glare and by softening the impact of the skyline increases the sense of intimacy.
Designer Keith Corlett

Right A trellis makes an effective screen for filtering the wind as well as a host for plants. It turns the salad garden into a secluded place to relax.

SOIL TYPES AND PLANTING

An understanding of the effect of different types of soil on plant growth and development is important, for this factor alone determines just what you can grow and where you can grow it. A little research at the survey stage will ensure that your garden flourishes rather than fails. In basic terms, there are two main considerations: the chemical makeup of the soil and its physical characteristics. Some soils are acidic, others alkaline; others are approximately halfway between the two and are described as neutral. Certain plants such as rhododendrons, camellias, and many heaths are acidic lovers, others such as clematis or broom enjoy an alkaline or limestone soil. It is almost impossible to grow acidic lovers on limestone and vice versa. Though some gardeners appear to relish the challenge of attempting to do so, their efforts are doomed to failure, since no matter how much you acidify a limestone soil the underlying alkalinity will work through and prevent normal development.

Very simple soil-testing kits or slightly more sophisticated soil-test meters that work by sliding a probe into the ground are available at good garden centers. Test the kind of soil you have at several places around the garden, since the acidity, or pH value, may vary. Be particularly on the alert if you know there are areas of imported topsoil, for these may well have quite a different pH from the rest of the garden. Note the results of your findings on the survey.

Most kits produce a color-coded result that can be related to the acidity of the soil. A low result, below a pH of 7, is acidic, while figures above this are alkaline: 7 is neutral and suitable for a wide range of plants. Most kits also list plants that are suitable for a particular kind of soil.

Soils also vary in their physical structure, being described as light or heavy. Sandy, easily-worked soils are light, while clays, which are more difficult to dig, are heavy. The workability of the soil has no bearing on its chemical makeup. Most important is the distinction between fertile topsoil and infertile subsoil. Topsoil is the upper layer, which can be light or heavy. It consists of broken-down rock particles to which organic matter has been added by the decomposition of plants and other decayed material known as humus. The ideal topsoil is humus-rich and easily worked. Plants need topsoil as a growing medium, and an ideal depth is 18in/450mm, though in fact the depth may vary from virtually nothing in a rocky area to more generous amounts in a rich alluvial river valley.

Subsoil is the layer beneath the topsoil that you find by deep digging. It is infertile and cannot support plant growth. If ever you have occasion to remove the topsoil – for example, when excavating a pond – set it carefully aside for use elsewhere in the garden. Never dump subsoil over topsoil, as happens only too frequently on building sites. This makes the soil virtually impossible to work, and the only practical solution is to get rid of it and replace it with clean topsoil.

Below Woodland gardens typically enjoy acidic soil. Here, a camellia and a tree fern, both acidic-loving plants, make an attractive combination in a shady corner, the fern's feathery foliage providing a good contrast with the glossy rounded leaves of the camellia. Both are growing well, clearly relishing the sheltered position and rich soil.

FROM SIMPLE SURVEY TO SCALE PLAN

Assess back and front gardens separately, and divide large gardens into manageable sections. Working roughly to scale, draw a basic outline plan. Begin with the profile of the back or front of the house, showing the position of doors and windows, then draw the garden boundaries. Now indicate the position of services (manholes and drains) and of major features. These might include a terrace, lawn, planting beds, paths, and structures, such as sheds or greenhouses. Mark the position of established trees, noting their spread or canopy, and, if relevant, including those in neighboring gardens. By straightforward measurement, by triangulation or offsets, establish the relative positions of all these features and enter the measurements on your outline plan. Annotate the plan with your observations of other important characteristics of the site.

You will need

A 100ft/30m flexible tape
A 15ft/5m steel tape
Several bamboo stakes
Metal spikes (for measuring curves)
Short metal pins (for holding tapes in position)
Clipboard, pencil, pad of paper
Level and flat board (3ft/1m square) for measuring long slopes

Measuring the garden

If the site is complicated, employ a professional surveyor: it is expensive, but worth it. In straightforward situations, most measurements can be taken from two base lines, one running across, the other down the garden. In our example, we have used three base lines, two of them running down the garden from the sides of the house. Also some measurements have been taken from the side boundaries.

1 Attach one end of the tape to a side boundary close to the house A. Extend it to the opposite boundary B and leave it lying on the ground. Check that it is parallel to the house by measuring out to it from either end of the house.

2 Go back to the start and work your way along the tape, noting on your outline sketch the distance from the boundary of the edge of the building, doors, and windows. Use the steel rule to measure projections from the house or low walls.

3 Attach the tape against the house, run it to the bottom of the garden C-D and check distances and features off this base line in the same way. Repeat for E-F. If the tape is not long enough, mark its end point with a bamboo stake. Reel in the tape, position it against the stake, and start measuring again, noting this "change point" on your plan.

Measuring curves

You may need to show a curve, such as that of a boundary or path, on your scale plan. To do this, first take measurements on site in the following way:

1 Locate two fixed points, at the beginning and end of the curve, by triangulation if necessary, and mark them with pins in the ground.

2 Stretch your tape between these points. Along this base line, at regular intervals, push a spike into the ground.

3 Measure the distance at right angles between each spike and the curve. Note the distances on your outline sketch. This information is easily transferred to the scale drawing as described on p.39.

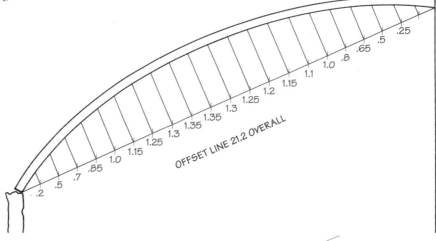

Triangulation

Pinpoint by triangulation the position of a feature, such as a tree, that cannot be readily and accurately measured off from a base line. Measure the distance out to the tree from two points, such as the corners of the house (E and G in our example), and note them on the sketch. They will enable you to draw two intersecting arcs that show the exact position of the tree on the scale drawing (see p.39).

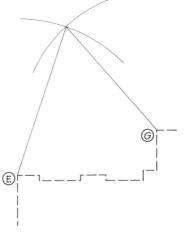

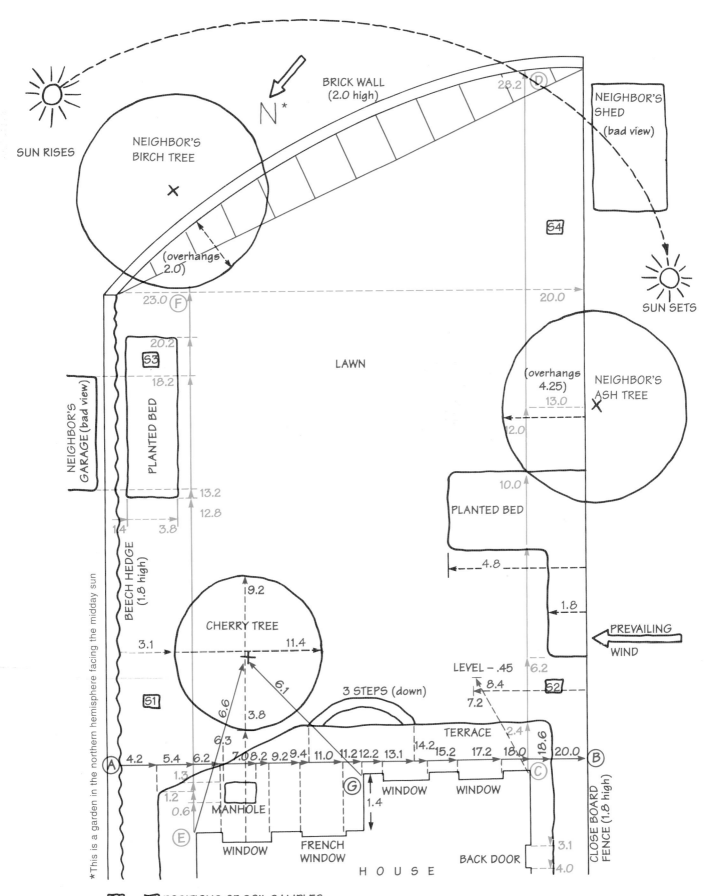

SUN RISES

NEIGHBOR'S
BIRCH TREE

BRICK WALL
(2.0 high)

N*

28.2 D

NEIGHBOR'S
SHED
(bad view)

S4

SUN SETS

(overhangs
2.0)

23.0 F

20.0

NEIGHBOR'S
GARAGE (bad view)

20.2

S3

18.2

LAWN

(overhangs
4.25)

13.0

NEIGHBOR'S
ASH TREE

PLANTED BED

2.0

13.2

12.8

1.4   3.8

10.0

PLANTED BED

4.8

BEECH HEDGE
(1.8 high)

1.8

9.2

PREVAILING
WIND

CHERRY TREE

3.1   11.4

LEVEL − .45

6.2

6.1

8.4

S2

6.6

3.8

7.2

2.4

6.3

3 STEPS (down)

TERRACE

18.6

S1

4.2   5.4   6.2   7.0 8.2 9.2 9.4   11.0 11.2 12.2 13.1 14.2 15.2   17.2 18.0 18.6 20.0 B

A

G

1.3

WINDOW   WINDOW

1.2

1.4

0.6   MANHOLE

E

WINDOW

FRENCH
WINDOW

BACK DOOR

3.1

4.0

CLOSE BOARD
FENCE (1.8 high)

H O U S E

*This is a garden in the northern hemisphere facing the midday sun

S1 - S4 POSITIONS OF SOIL SAMPLES

Measuring down a slope

Slopes that fall or rise up to 10ft/3m can be measured by a simple combination of tape and eye. Steeper slopes or complicated sites are best left to professional surveyors. The method of sighting described here should not be employed more than twice on one slope or inaccuracy will creep in. Before you start, measure your own height from foot to eye level.

1 Work from a level point close to the house, such as the floor of a terrace.
2 Walk down the slope until, when you turn back to look at the terrace, your eyeline is horizontal with the floor. If you have to crouch slightly, because the distance is short, use a steel tape to measure your foot to eye distance.
3 Note on your sketch your own foot to eye height and the distance between you and the fixed point. This shows the gradient of the slope.

4 A long slope may need more than one sighting, so you need to make another level: a board about 3ft/1m square would be suitable. Rest the back edge on the slope at the first sighting point and prop up the front edge with two pegs in the ground. Use a level to check the board is positioned correctly. Take a second sighting from the level edge of the board. Add this to the result of your first sighting to find the total fall over the distance you have walked. Mark the bottom point on your survey.

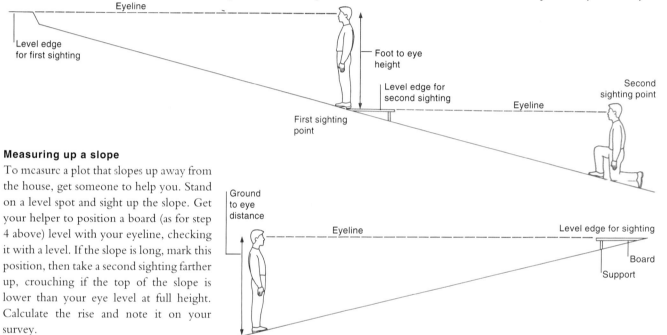

Measuring up a slope

To measure a plot that slopes up away from the house, get someone to help you. Stand on a level spot and sight up the slope. Get your helper to position a board (as for step 4 above) level with your eyeline, checking it with a level. If the slope is long, mark this position, then take a second sighting farther up, crouching if the top of the slope is lower than your eye level at full height. Calculate the rise and note it on your survey.

You will need

A clean flat work surface
A sheet of graph/squared paper
A sheet of tracing paper
Pencil, eraser, ruler
Drafting or Scotch Tape
A pair of compasses
A square

Drawing the plan to scale

Observing and recording information about your home, garden, and surrounding neighborhood is an enlightening experience. Now you can look on them with a new, sharpened awareness and, thanks to this analytical assessment, new ideas begin to emerge about how you can use and enjoy the garden.

The first step toward designing or redesigning a space that works for all who use it is to translate the results of your survey into an accurate scale plan. This means miniaturizing the garden plan so that it fits onto a manageable sheet of paper. For most gardens, a scale of 1:100 is appropriate. Thus if you are working in metric measurements, 1cm on the drawing equals 1m on the ground. For a very small garden, 1:50 would be preferable, with 2cm on the drawing equaling 1m on the ground. If you are working in Imperial, the nearest equivalent scales are $^1/_8$ in=1ft (which is 1:96) or $^1/_4$ in=1ft (1:48). Metric measurements were used for the survey and the plan opposite, which was drawn to a scale of 1:100.

Making a scale drawing

1 Calculate roughly how big your drawing is going to be, and choose a sheet of graph paper of an appropriate size. A garden 30m long and 20m wide would then measure 30x20cm, using a scale of 1:100.

2 Secure the paper to the work surface with drafting or Scotch Tape. Position the tracing paper over it and secure with drafting tape.

3 Start near the bottom left-hand corner of the sheet, allowing a wide margin for your annotation, and number the graph squares across and up the page according to the system of measurement you are using and the scale you have selected. In our example, this is 20 across, 23 up the left-hand side and 29 up the right-hand side.

4 First draw in the house, following the measurements off the first base line A-B. At 1:100, 18.6m scales off at 18.6cm, and so on.

5 Repeat the exercise, at right angles to the house, up the garden, plotting the position of features noted on base lines C-D and E-F.

6 Identify the exact position of triangulated features. Read off one triangulation distance from the survey, say from E in the drawing on p.37, and translate this to a scaled measurement. Extend your compasses accordingly, place the point on E and draw an arc. Repeat for the other measurement, in this case from point G. Where the arcs intersect is the exact position of the tree (see p.36).

7 Plot the curve of the boundary. First establish the ends of the curve, by triangulation if necessary, then draw a line between them. Scale the base line off at 1cm (1m) intervals and, using your square, draw lines at right angles to plot the offset distances. Join these points together to accurately indicate the curve (see p.36).

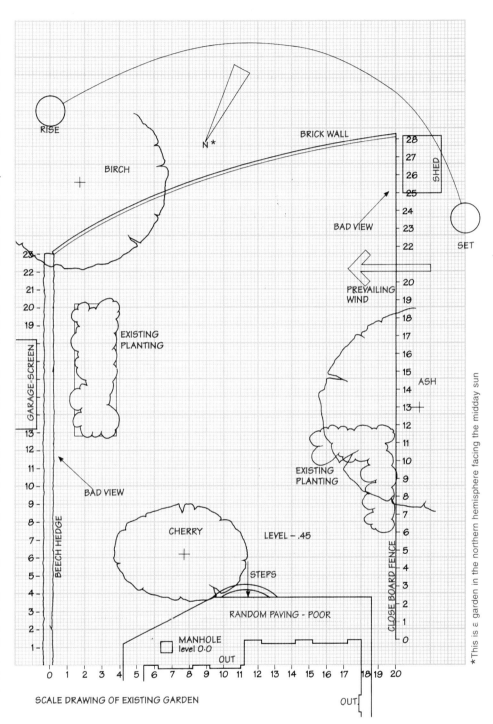

SCALE DRAWING OF EXISTING GARDEN

*This is a garden in the northern hemisphere facing the midday sun

Once you have transferred all relevant notes to your scale drawing, it is complete. You are now a surveyor of the highest order, and you know your plot backward. Take photocopies of the drawing, and file the original safely away. You will be using a photocopy as a basis for the next design stage, in which you experiment with various possible layouts for your redesigned garden. This is where the really creative work begins.

DESIGNING
WITH STYLE

Good design is about simplicity and fitness for purpose – whether you opt for a formal, informal, or combination of styles. These different ways of realizing a design are explained and evaluated in this chapter, with a wealth of examples to help you determine your own approach. This should meet all your needs, reflect your own personality and preferences, and be in harmony with your surroundings. A successful design can be achieved by the observation of some simple rules relating to the manipulation of space and the contribution of color, pattern, and texture.

One of the most rewarding aspects of making a detailed survey is that it enables you to look at your plot with fresh eyes, often from an entirely new perspective. Some parts of the garden, you may realize, have potential that has not yet been exploited; others may never have quite worked in the way you had hoped, and now you understand why. By this time, you have a clear idea of the various functions you want your garden to fulfill, and you can begin translating your needs into a final design.

As you work on the garden layout, roughing-in particular areas to accommodate particular activities, you are creating a pattern – in the first instance, on paper. Whether the pattern is based on rigid geometry and symmetry or is more fluid and freeform depends on many factors, some of which will be governed by the survey information you have gathered. It will also be driven by what you want, what you like and dislike, the amount of maintenance you are prepared to undertake, your budget, and, just as important, the style of your house and the area in which it is built. If the plan is to succeed in practice, it must reflect all these considerations. Indeed, the purpose of the plan is to do this. This is what fitness for purpose is all about.

Before you can formulate precise patterns, however, you need to think of the layout in more general terms. Use a photocopy of your scale drawing and some sheets of tracing paper to experiment, with all the relevant information at your fingertips, before you commit yourself to a final design. It is easy to work over the base plan, first quickly tracing off the outline of the garden. Sketch in sitting and barbecue areas close to the house, vegetable lot farther away, and so on, always bearing in mind that your aim is to link the garden in visual and physical terms with the house – its interior as well as exterior. Indicate, too, the possible position of important features – a building, pond, or rocky outcrop. You can use any number of sheets, working through as many ideas as you want, sliding them one under or over the other, as overlays or underlays, while you explore alternatives. Always remember that experiencing a garden, just as much as a house, is an exercise in moving through space, and that a garden seen at a glance is less interesting than one that is discovered, stage by stage, as you move through the composition. For the moment, it is enough simply to indicate possible positions and routes through and between areas; they can be firmed up later.

Even the largest design, if it is to work, must be strongly conceived to embrace an overall, coherent, style. It is important to decide on this at an early stage, because to a large extent it determines the layout and distribution of different elements within the garden framework. Your thoughts on style and the information gleaned from the survey play crucial roles in the development of a design. Do not be tempted to crystallize any ideas too soon; try as many rough layouts as you like until you find one that satisfies all your needs.

A formal approach

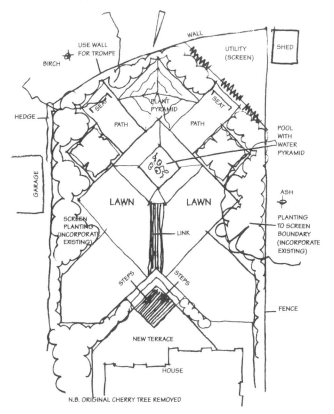

Structured informality

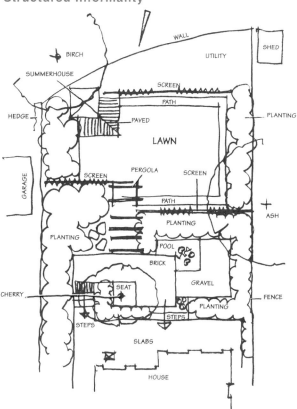

An informal approach

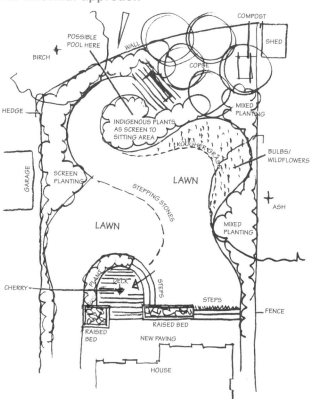

Setting a style Taking as a basis the sample plot that we surveyed and drew to scale in Chapter 2, I have drawn rough layouts for three very different treatments: one is strictly formal, and in this geometry and symmetry prevail. The other two explore degrees of informality – from the structured to the freeform. Whatever the style, plan your garden around your favorite activities. Play areas, barbecues, and vegetable plots should be integral parts of the design. Indicate roughly where they and other major features – decks, pools, paths, and terraces – will go. I eventually worked these rough layouts up into the final designs shown on pp.108–109.

YOUR GARDEN STYLE

Style is subjective. At best, the style of a garden reflects the character of those who live in it as well as that of its locality; at worst, it panders to fashion, which is always transient. Do not be seduced by gardens in glossy magazines or books, on television or at garden shows. Take inspiration from them, certainly, but do not be tempted to copy them wholesale: they were built to suit a set of circumstances entirely different from your own. A wildlife garden may look irresistible on the page, with an appealing air of neglect, but the reality might prove a real burden in terms of maintenance. The important thing is to find a style and solution that suits you and your lifestyle.

Your first general thoughts might focus on whether your preference, your needs, and, of course, the style of your house suggest a formal or informal approach. While a large enough garden might contain more than one style, do not be tempted to produce a stylistic cocktail that is likely to be unsatisfying on all levels. Here we can learn a lesson from the Victorians, who attempted to cram every conceivable plant, ornament, and style into their precious, but limited, outdoor space. Enthusiastic but indiscriminate, they reproduced a hodgepodge or pastiche of earlier styles that not only betrayed their lack of understanding of the originals but were also unsatisfactory in both practical and visual terms. The lesson that we can learn from the Victorians, one of the most important about any form of design, is that you should never create a style or design for its own sake. Simplicity is the key to any worthwhile composition, while overcomplication is the antithesis.

A formal approach

Although formality has nothing necessarily to do with a specific date or time, when we talk about formal gardens we tend to think in historical terms. Formal patterns are based on a straightforward grid, where balanced shapes can easily be worked out. If the date or style of your house indicates a controlled, geometric approach and this also seems appropriate to the site, your personality and the functions you want your garden to fulfill, there is a long tradition to which you can turn for inspiration. In ancient Rome, as leisure time became more important, houses often included an enclosed central courtyard that had developed from the *hortus* or vegetable plot. This was a private area, often surrounded by a portico or peristyle, where the family could stroll in the shade. Planted with shrubs and flowers, dotted with fountains to add to the feeling of calm and coolness, and often including a small shrine, the courtyard became the classic outdoor room, in perfect harmony with the house itself. In the great Renaissance gardens, the geometry of the building extended out into the landscape, where the links between the house and garden were evident in the lines of trimmed parterres and formal allées.

Below The fusion of indoors and out is perfectly expressed in the design of Moorish gardens, where tiled floors unite the two. Cool, shady cloisters surround this formal inner courtyard at the Villa Taylor in Marrakesh, which is enlivened by the sound and movement of a central water feature. Planting is kept simple, so that it does not vie for attention with the intricate detailing of the floor.

Such gardens have a soothing, timeless air.

Geometry and symmetry also governed the design of Moorish gardens – cool, refreshing, private retreats from the heat, dust, and wind of the desert. Traditionally designed as rectangular courtyards surrounded by the house itself, they were divided into four by paths or water channels with a pool, fountain, or pavilion providing a central focal point. Like the Roman garden, the Moorish garden was quintessentially an outdoor room closely connected through porticoes, doorways, and windows with the interior of the house, a connection further emphasized by the continuity of paving between the two. This quadripartite design has been echoed countless times in formal gardens throughout the Western world. Apart from visiting surviving gardens, such as those at the Alhambra in Granada, you might also turn for inspiration to the famous Persian garden carpets, which show plans of the gardens in elaborate decorative detail.

In today's small formal gardens, a projecting bay or a doorway might form the basis of a central axis running down the garden. At a point along this line, marked perhaps by a pool, sundial, or pergola, a cross axis could be designed at right angles, with regular features, such as planted beds, parterres, urns, and trimmed trees, to either side. Details, as in formal rooms, might be set out in a regular pattern: chairs or alcoves either side of a chimneypiece in a living room, for example, could be translated outdoors into urns flanking a gateway.

Formal gardens are essentially ordered affairs. Even when plants are allowed to spill over onto paths or paving to soften their geometry, their outline is controlled.

Below Within a formal layout, hedges and boxwood-edged beds form a strong framework into which planting and other features are worked. Here the ground plan is reinforced with a ceiling that further contains the space. The pergola naturally leads the eye past the cross axis toward the entrance into the next garden room.
Designer Ian Pollard

Pages 48-49 Different house styles and sites suggest contrasting ways of integrating ponds in small gardens. The formality of an elliptical lily pool, perfectly aligned with the central axis of the house, is offset and softened by a relaxed approach in the planting. In an even smaller space, an L-shaped pond is the dominant feature of an asymmetrical layout.
Landscape Architects: Wolfgang Oehme and James Anthony van Sweden

Opposite A shallow step staggered around an old established tree underlines its importance as a feature, while introducing a lively feeling of movement. An architectural treatment, with brick paving, close to the house gives way to a more informal approach beyond the decorative wooden fence.
Designer James Hitchmough

Below In this detail of one of my own asymmetric garden designs, decks, paving bricks, water, and plants set up interesting spatial relationships, achieving balance without symmetry.

Since plants, by nature, resist such treatment, strictly formal gardens require the attention of a keen gardener. They suit people with an ordered outlook: they suggest that you walk in particular directions, and their pattern enforces a leisurely pace. Well-suited to a sedate game of croquet, the formal lawn does not invite rowdy kickabouts or enthusiastic Frisbee throwing, so the formal approach, in a garden of average size, is unlikely to be suitable for a family with growing children.

Because they are strictly controlled, remaining much the same over a long period of time, formal gardens have an air of permanence and stability. Their unchanging nature may also mean that, while they are demanding, they may in fact be less so than informal gardens, where there are usually more variables and maintenance follows a less defined and regular sequence.

While there are many historical sources of ideas for formal layouts, the composition need not be traditional or retrospective. Formal design can be treated in a thoroughly Modernist or post-Modernist way. And if your garden is large enough, you could include one or two less formal areas (see p.51).

Structured informality

You may wish to give your garden an obvious sense of structure without the rigid symmetry of an absolutely formal garden. In this case, you could adopt a balanced but asymmetrical approach that falls somewhere between the strictly formal and the totally informal. The key elements in this sort of layout are not mirrored as in a rigidly formal design but are related in a more subtle way. To help clarify the concept, imagine the balance of a formal layout as being maintained by two equal weights set at the same distance from a fulcrum. In an asymmetrical layout, balance is maintained by using different weights at different distances from the fulcrum. In such a plan, a terrace may be laid out so that interlocking raised beds on one side balance the visual weight of a large paved area on the other. Farther down the garden, a tree group may offset a major feature, such as a summerhouse.

Asymmetry was an important tool for the Modernists, and in the work of garden designers such as Thomas Church and Garrett Eckbo such compositions evolved into the perfect outdoor living space (see pp.7-9). At the same time, in the 1930's and 1940's, when landscape designers and architects were exploring the boundaries of geometry in a totally fresh way and redistributing features in a more fluid and freethinking fashion, painters such as Mondrian, Kandinsky, and Klee were engaged in a similar exercise. In fact, a painting by Mondrian that is divided into beautiful geometric patterns can be perfectly translated into a garden design, the different areas of color being divided into paving, water, and planting; my own garden (see pp.140-143) is an extension of this idea. This kind of crossfertilization of ideas is not only richly productive but also helps break down divisions between the various disciplines.

The informal approach

The best features of informal gardening, on a grand scale, were epitomized in the English landscape school of the eighteenth century. Rejecting the geometry that suggests control, they embraced a far more relaxed and natural style, taking their cues from naturalistic French painting. There were serpentine lakes, vast sweeps of lawn running up to the great house, and, in the far reaches of the garden, naturalistic woodlands. These grand gardens were in a truly indigenous English style, probably the only one, and they provided inspiration for generations of landscape and garden designers to come.

The informal style today can be said to be anything that is *not* formal. The degree of informality can range from the inherent geometry of the asymmetric style (see p.46) to the far greater informality of the freeform wildlife or naturalistic garden. A natural look is often the aim of a truly informal design: geometry has no place in it, and rigid boundaries are disguised, if possible, with abundant vegetation. The shapes of planting beds and lawns are fluid, paths meander, perhaps through meadow grass. Informal gardens are designed to include surprises: screens, bushes, and plants hide one part of the garden from another. These are gardens to enjoy on many levels, inviting participation, whether of an energetic or relaxed nature. Beguilingly naturalistic in appearance, they nonetheless depend on a strong design concept.

A different kind of informality is expressed in Japanese gardens, which demonstrate a natural understanding and a taming of landscape within the confines of a small plot. Creativity allied to profound understanding and consummate skill in the use of both hard and soft landscape materials results in gardens that are not only beautiful but also totally fit for their purpose – contemplation. The enjoyment of a garden on a meditative level is important, whatever its style. An ivy garden planted with just that species, a rock, boulder, or gravel garden, a water garden, or bog garden – all are planned primarily to be enjoyable visual experiences.

A fusion of styles

If elements of both formality and informality appeal to you, one way of combining them in a practical working composition might be to follow a set design sequence. Formality could prevail in areas close to the house, with the lines of the terrace and, perhaps, raised beds and planting extending the angularity of the building. From the terrace, a path could sweep around a lawn, with areas of planting built up in an asymmetrical pattern linking back to the terrace. Beyond, separated by a screen, there might be one or two more rooms that are completely informal. Here is the place for romantic retreats from the world at large, for wildlife gardens or simply for rough grass studded with buttercups in summer.

Opposite A mown path meanders past beds and rough grass naturalized with wildflowers. Informal compositions must be carefully planned, particularly in relation to movement through space. Here, planting determines the flow, much like that of a river.
Designer Mirabel Osler

Below Some outdoor rooms, such as this one in Australia, are made simply to delight the eye and refresh the spirit. The rhythmical, flowing shapes and varied textures of this Japanese-style garden invite gentle exploration.
Designer Polly Park

WORKING WITH SPACE

The creation of a garden inevitably means that you are working with, and designing in, a vertical as well as a horizontal plane. The latter, of course, may be underfoot or overhead (pergolas, awnings, canopies, etc). It is the character of the volume formed by this containment of space that determines both how you perceive and use outdoor rooms. Thus the manipulation of space is a key element in designing a garden.

There are a number of ways of changing the perception of space, making it appear larger, smaller, longer or shorter, as wished. It can be achieved through the skillful handling of pattern, color, and texture – in both the hard and soft landscape – or through visual tricks, such as the use of false perspective. Using lines that seem parallel but that actually narrow as they recede from a viewpoint, or elements that physically diminish as they recede, has the effect, if not overdone, of suggesting greater space (although looking back on this kind of visual trickery from the opposite end of the vista is odd!). Other trompe features, such as false perspective trellis and mirrors, can be used with discretion. These are discussed in greater detail in Chapter 5.

Desire lines

The points at which spaces are entered and left determine movement through them. Entry and exit points in the opposite corners of a rectangle encourage a diagonal route to be taken across it, while those at either end suggest a route directly up and down. Known by designers as desire lines, they indicate the quickest or easiest way across or through an area. Such routes can be modified in a number of ways: the position of walls, screens, or planting, contouring of the ground, or dramatic changes in level – all can deflect both feet and eye and dictate the line of paths to a considerable degree.

The imaginative manipulation of desire lines is one way of creating the elements of mystery, tension, and surprise that are essential ingredients of a successful garden. Curiosity is aroused, for example, by a path that curves away from a viewpoint and disappears behind a wing of planting or beneath a pergola. Tension mounts as you draw close to a gateway in a wall separating two garden rooms; as you pass through the gate or "tension point," tension is released, and you move on to the discovery of a new space.

Below left In an informal situation, directional emphasis may be more subtle. Here, stepping stones suggest a course continuing the curve of the pathway.

This Australian garden was originally created in the 1930's by the famous garden designer Edna Walling.

Below right In a rigidly designed space, entrances and exits are obvious, taking you through in an orderly manner. Here the framework is determined by low boxwood hedges that emphasize the shallow steps.
Designer Christopher Masson

Below left Impeccably laid pale precast concrete slabs make an excellent foil for both planting and shadows. Composed of rigidly geometric modules, a succession of rectangles, the floor pattern introduces an intriguing sense of movement to this outdoor room.
Designer John Plummer

Below right Stepping stones flow with the line of the raised bed and introduce a dynamic curve in an essentially minimalist composition. With pebbles providing a contrast in form, texture, and color, they make a strong visual impact.
Designer Michael Branch

THE EFFECT OF PATTERN

When you are satisfied with the general style and layout of the garden, you can begin to hone the pattern further. Now is the time to think more precisely about the size, shape, and character of the features you have penciled in on your plan and to consider how they are to be linked with one another. You need to determine, for example, the exact positioning of the pattern that physically forms a link with the house, aligning the corner of a paving slab, for example, with a precise point such as a corner of the building, French windows, or the edge of a sliding door. No one would think of misaligning a wallpaper pattern or setting an architrave around a door at an angle inside the house, yet garden paving often starts at an odd angle to the building, while paths, lawns, and other features run into one another in a haphazard and visually awkward way.

Close attention to pattern is vital if the room is to work and look its best, and this is as important in small-scale pattern as it is in the large-scale pattern of the ground plan. All pattern must have a purpose and should never be used simply for its own sake or to bolster a weak design. A restrained approach is likely to be the most successful: a busy pattern, whether in the hard landscape or in the planting, is likely to be restless in effect and visually counterproductive. At its best, pattern

enhances a particular surface or area and uses materials that are compatible with one another as well as appropriate in their setting. Such materials can often be seen in traditional situations, where intricate paving or wall details make a rich contribution to the setting. In terms of planting, the principle is the same: pattern – created by the controlled and carefully planned use of color, shape, or texture – must relate to the overall design and style of the garden.

Pattern has an important effect on our perception of space, and how we use it. For example, paving laid in courses or lines down a path tends to accelerate both feet and eye, but if laid across will have the reverse effect, slowing the view down. The same technique can be used to give the appearance of widening a narrow space. A diagonal pattern helps to increase the width of a garden visually, drawing the eye away from rectangular boundaries. The way a lawn is mown creates patterns that have a similar effect, and a mown pattern that leads around a sweeping corner helps to reinforce a feeling of mystery. Planting patterns, too, can alter our perception of space: broad drifts of different species make for a feeling of continuity and movement. On the largest scale, trees can be sheared to direct a view, while shadows cast by a mature tree produce informal patterns that swing across the garden through the day.

Below Similar patterns in both hard and soft landscapes are a feature of some of the most dramatic garden designs. Here the careful manipulation of hedges echoes the angles of the lumber. This beautifully thought-out asymmetrical study commands attention, now drawing the eye to the bust at the end of the vista, now drawing it strongly to the left, over the pyramidally trimmed hedge. *Designer Gus Lieber*

USING COLOR CREATIVELY

Color is one of the most important elements at the garden designer's disposal. It can be used to suggest a mood, whether restrained or romantic. It can be used to increase or decrease the feeling of space or provide a theme around which your outdoor room, or series of rooms, is planned. In terms of both hard and soft landscape, color plays an important role in reflecting your personality and conveying your individuality to others.

Forget the color wheel. I have been unable to fathom it since I left college. So, don't allow yourself to be bemused by complex theories about the juxtaposition of colors. Over the last twenty-five years, I have planned increasingly beautiful gardens using a few very simple design rules, and, if they work for me, they can also work for you.

Above Explosions of primary colors on fences, arches, railings, and gates pepper the Long Island garden of artist-gardener Robert Dash. Designed to punctuate the garden's winter monochrome with flashes of brilliance, these vivid hues make an equally striking contribution in lusher, greener seasons.

Robert Dash likes to change the colors often: this ever-open gate, a vibrant yellow in spring, may be transformed with a coat of brash bright blue for summer.

Right The clear luminous yellows of alchemilla and euphorbia flood this shaded terrace with light. To wrap a sitting area in yellow is visually and psychologically warming.
Designer John Brookes

When planning rooms inside the house you probably think around a color scheme, making sure that wall coverings, flooring, and furnishings work together: outside, these same considerations are equally important. Professional designers always ascertain which colors their clients like and dislike; ask yourself the same question, bearing in mind the color schemes that work for you inside the home.

An overall color scheme for the garden embraces the hard and soft landscape as well as the incidentals, such as furnishings, pots, and statuary. If that color scheme also flows into or leads out from the house, then so much the better. In terms of furnishings, for example, it obviously makes sense to extend a color scheme from inside to out. Awnings, seat covers, and cushions can all take their cue from adjoining areas.

One of the most important influences on color is the light in which it is seen:

Below The white of the delicate wrought-iron seat provides the perfect foil to a harmonious composition of greens and yellows.

Remember that bright sunlight helps to tone down a strong color, while on a dull day it will have far more brilliance. Thus a design like this works well for a number of different light values.

the stronger the light, the paler a particular hue will appear. In Mediterranean and tropical regions, where the natural light is brilliant, people use strong vibrant colors not only in their homes but also in their gardens. Those same colors in a more temperate climate, with softer light values, can look brash and out of place. This is why the pastel ranges look their best in temperate zones and why hardy perennial or herbaceous planting plans are so popular and effective. The question of light values also has a bearing on our perception of space. An open unshaded area looks expansive, while a darker space, perhaps overhung by trees, is foreshortened. So you can increase or decrease the feeling of space by removing or casting shadow.

Because spaces outside the home are often bigger than rooms inside, there is greater scope for using different color ranges, particularly if the garden is

Below Flouting all conventions, these brilliant hues – the strong purple of *Pontederia cordata* with its luminous green-yellow leaves, the bright red board fence, and the blue deck – are used with such confidence and conviction that they work well, even in the softer light of northern Europe. *Designer Henk Weijers*

subdivided into different areas. As a general rule, hot colors draw the eye: a group of pots planted with strong primary colors placed at the end of a vista immediately attracts the attention, at the expense of everything else on the way. This is fine if you want to divert the gaze from a less pleasant view, but if it is used indiscriminately this approach can produce a series of unrelated focal points that make for an unsettled picture.

Most home decorators are familiar with the idea of dark colors advancing and pale colors receding: the same principle can be applied outside to alter perceptions of size and to lengthen or foreshorten views. A slope rising away from a viewpoint, for example, tends to be visually foreshortened, while one that falls away has a feeling of spaciousness; a pale planting design is a far better choice than a dark one for a small upwardly sloping garden.

Below A vibrant red is introduced as a counterpoint into a predominantly cool scheme using its complementary green and a combination of pastels. Without it, the composition might look somewhat bland. The red is tempered by gray, an indispensable harmonizer in any situation.

Below left The imaginative interplay of rich textures and patterns turns a path into an eye-catching, decorative feature. Stone slabs set in a sea of perfectly laid cobbles direct foot and eye to the superb wrought-iron gate at Cranbourne Manor in Hampshire, England.
Designer Lady Salisbury

Below right The tight domelike habit and springy texture of helxine beautifully complements and offsets smooth, flat, hard stone.
Designer Jim Matsuo

EXPLOITING TEXTURES

The contribution of texture in the garden's hard and soft landscapes is visual as well as tactile. Whether a surface is smooth or deeply furrowed affects not only the sense of touch but also that of sight, since light striking the face of paving bricks or plants casts an increasingly dark shadow according to the depth of indentation. This in turn has a significant effect on the perception of space. Visually, the flat surface engenders feelings of space, while the deeper shadows of a more textured surface make it more dominant. The boundaries of a garden or yard enveloped in heavily textured foliage, for example, tend to be drawn inward and make the area feel smaller. Depending, therefore, on whether you want to increase or decrease the impression of space you might opt for a smooth rendered wall as opposed to a rough-textured one, or for a plain boarded fence rather than woven wattle hurdles with their richly textured surface. Texture also affects our progress through a space: a perfectly flat paved surface encourages faster foot traffic, while an uneven cobbled surface slows or deters it.

Textures can, of course, be varied and juxtaposed, creating visual variation and interesting patterns as well as a change of pace. Courses of textured brick can be set within an overall surface of smooth precast concrete slabs, small smooth cobbles used as a contrast infill among rectangular Tennessee fieldstone.

The juxtaposition of various textures of foliage is a vital ingredient of planting design, providing interest over a far longer period than flowers alone. Glorious contrasts can be achieved in the planting: one such might be the juxtaposition of the deeply veined leaves of the wild rhubarb *Rheum palmatum rubrum* with the smooth swordlike leaves of Siberian iris.

Of course, hard and soft surfaces can never be kept separate in the garden, and there is continual interplay between them. Grass, chamomile, and thyme may add to the ground-cover palette, while trees create their own textures at a higher level.

You can eventually begin to weave the incidental punctuation of furniture and ornament into the background texture of hard and soft landscape, while always respecting the overall theme.

Below left

At Chenies Manor in Buckingham-shire, England, delicate gray fronds of artemisia contrast strikingly with the broad-leaved hosta and simple white begonia flowers.

Below right

Different textures – bleached slatted seats set on smooth stone paving stones against a rugged stone wall – enliven an essentially monochromatic design.

CREATING THE FRAMEWORK

The framework of the outdoor room not only provides a perimeter and establishes internal divisions but also determines the way we move about the space and how we furnish each area. Practical and aesthetic considerations operate here just as much as inside the house. Outdoors, however, the advantages of greater space, changes in level, good views, and the very real bonus of fresh air, sunlight, and a living palette present the possibility of different and exciting design solutions. Choose materials for the walls, floors, and ceiling of your outdoor rooms so that, as well as working on a practical level, they look good, reflecting the style and purpose of your garden plan.

Previous pages A strong framework, built up from rectangles, needs well-chosen plants to soften its geometry. Here split-level beds, cascading with flowers and foliage, provide balance and counterpoint. The mirror, cleverly positioned behind the pool, doubles the depth of part of this garden, which is also shown on p.81.
Designer Barbara Thomas

The choice of materials for the framework can be overwhelming, as any trip to a good garden center or building supply store will bear out. If you are likely to be seduced by the idea of complex paving patterns for the garden's floor, by theatrical trelliswork or exotic arches for its walls and transition points, or by an elaborate awning for the ceiling, bring to mind the design criteria I have discussed: resolve to keep things simple, use materials sensitively, and choose them to link the garden with the house and with its surrounding area.

The ideal garden uses a combination of both hard and soft landscaping to achieve balance and interest year-round. The hard landscape embraces the paving, paths, steps, ramps, and other "hard" incidentals of the garden. Hedges, lawns, expanses of water, and ground-cover planting create the soft landscape. It is the hard landscape that largely governs the ground plan and takes the lion's share, often as much as 75 percent, of the budget. This is why it is important to prepare an accurate plan before you embark on any project; you can then make equally accurate estimates of the quantities of materials needed and, if necessary, phase the work over a long period. Properly installed, hard landscaping should last a lifetime; the effect and pleasure it gives is, of course, instant.

THE WALLS

The external walls define the boundaries or outer limits of a garden. Internal walls and screens are used to subdivide the plot, creating smaller rooms within the overall space, and to guide you through it. If handled well, subdividing a garden actually makes it feel larger, because of the introduction of elements of mystery and surprise. Internal divisions can be made not only from the same materials that are used for boundaries but also from lightweight materials that allow a partial view through. Both external and internal walls can provide privacy and shelter, act to some extent as barriers to noise, and can be used to support climbing plants.

Remember that walls and fences are a backdrop that can be softened or further patterned with planting. A large-leafed vine against a narrow board fence or the delicate tracery of a Japanese maple against a smooth, white-painted wall make strong decorative focal points. Shadows, too, whether cast by or onto the boundary, play a part. The chevron shadows of a slatted fence, the dark band cast by a solid wall, or the perforated pattern of honeycomb brickwork all have their own character and add a further dimension to the outdoor room.

Not all walls, fences, and hedges need to be a constant height or have a constant line. Add interest to the boundary by staggering the height of a wall, curving the upper edge of a fence or scalloping the top of a hedge. A curve leads the eye in a particular direction. Gaps or gates offer a fresh vista or the promise of a new area to be discovered.

You may be lucky in that you move into a home where beautiful stone or brick walls are already in position, or where there are sturdy fences or well-grown hedges. If you need to provide your own, emphasize the link between house and garden. You can do this by choosing the same materials, brick of the same color, for example; or, if you have a large picture window dividing house and garden, by painting a wall to pick up on a color scheme used inside or by planting it with vines to echo the indoor plants.

As a general rule, natural materials are more expensive than manmade: stone has the advantage, however, of individuality and of suiting a situation where other natural materials predominate. In many places, manmade materials are the obvious choice if you are attempting to link house and garden. It may be, however, that you need to complement natural materials but cannot afford them. In this case, it is usually sensible to opt for a quite different, nonnatural material at a fraction of the cost. Beware of using an artificial material, such as reconstituted stone (a mixture of ground stone and cement) that mimics a natural one. While some reconstituted stone blocks are good copies of natural stone, most can readily be distinguished from the real thing. Smooth-faced concrete blocks, on the other hand, in the same color range as natural stone look straightforward and honest and can stand as design features in their own right.

Opposite The character of a wall – the material it is made of and the way it is constructed – should be in tune with its surroundings. Where stone outcrops naturally, it is the logical and best choice. In this Los Angeles garden designed by Garrett Eckbo, a wall with stones set in a random pattern and bonded with mortar harmonizes with the adjoining paving as well as with the rugged rocky site.

Below A work of art in itself, this drystone wall is "brought to courses" with stones of varying widths creating a delightful, informal rhythm. The hand of a skilled craftsman is evident.

Above Dressed stone is expensive, long-lasting, and looks superb. These blocks of a delicately hued local sandstone acquire a soft golden glow with age. They have been "pounced" or "sparrow picked" to produce a stippled shadow pattern. A double white camellia espaliered along the horizontal joints introduces an unusual and lively dimension.

Natural stone

Stone ranges from soft, sedimentary rocks, such as sandstone or slate, to harder igneous types that include granite, flints, and grits. Its strong, local character makes stone particularly suitable for use in the area from which it comes. In general, the farther stone is transported, the more out of place it looks and the more expensive it becomes.

Another factor affecting its price is the degree to which the stone is shaped or "dressed." Rough-hewn stone suitable for an informal look in a rural location is cheaper than stone that has been sawn or cut into blocks. Use dressed stone for a more architectural effect in a city, or to mark the boundaries of a fine stone-built rural house.

Rough-hewn stone

Rough-hewn stone is often used by local craftsmen in drystone walling of various types throughout the world. As its name suggests, no mortar is used to bond the wall together, and for this reason you should not build a drystone wall more than a yard/meter high. Foundations are minimal – usually compacted soil or large pieces of stone. The wall is built so that it tapers in or "batters" slightly toward the top. "Through" stones run right through the wall to tie the construction together, while the coping, or top course, usually consists of stones set on edge. Drystone walls can either be built with a random pattern, or "brought to courses," where the bond is more regular. This would be the right choice for a wall adjoining a stone house, where the walls of the house are normally coursed.

Different techniques are used in different regions, and construction is a skilled job, normally best left to craftsmen. Owing to their relatively low height, dry-

Left Roughly laid, with stones placed randomly rather than "brought to courses," this informal drystone wall has enormous visual strength. With a simple coping of large flat stones, it works perfectly in this setting, where a low barrier is required to contain the vegetable plot while allowing views across the lake.
Designer Edwina von Gal

Opposite below Large pieces of cut stone laid with mortar provide necessary extra strength at the corners of these drystone walls. Each spans three or four courses, and they are bonded in alternate directions.
Designer Ian Pollard

stone walls offer little in the way of privacy, but they will keep pets and children in and can embrace a view. Fill their crevices with pockets of soil, which you can plant with a wide range of alpine and trailing plants.

For a taller and more durable wall, use the same stone with mortar joints and a coping to prevent water seeping into them. Sound concrete foundations or footings are essential, and take great care with the pointing to ensure neat joints. I have built such walls around my own house, using as a coping a dark blue engineering brick that picks up the color of the slate roof of the house.

To make a boundary in an open landscape, consider building a ha-ha, or stone-faced ditch. These became popular during the eighteenth century to keep livestock in without interrupting the view. Today, if space and finances permit, it is a more attractive and less obtrusive alternative than the overused post-and-rail fence.

Another traditional boundary is built by constructing a wide earth bank tapered toward the top and faced with local stone. Sods are laid between the stones, and these provide the opportunity for wildflowers to seed themselves and cover the bank. Consider building such a bank if you are in the right sort of rural setting.

Dressed stone

Walls made from dressed or cut stone blocks look superb, in traditional as well as high-tech settings. They must be craftsman-built, and are very expensive, but they will last hundreds of years. Regular courses of similar-sized blocks will form a no-nonsense, low-key background to any garden. If you vary the width of the courses and rake back the horizontal lines of the pointing to form a shadow line, the wall will have far greater directional emphasis, leading the eye down its face and along its length.

Below Confidently flouting the rule not to mix too many materials, this wall combines knapped flint comfortably in a random pattern with brick and stone. Brick coping prevents weather penetration.
Designer Jan Martinez

Knapped flint

For this type of walling, split flint – a particularly hard stone – is set in mortar. In
the best examples, the flints are woven into intricate patterns and the mortar does
not show. Because of their irregular nature, knapped-flint walls are often built in
panels that are framed and backed with stone or brick. Copings vary, but some use
old pantiles or even thatch, which adds enormously to their character. If you want
a knapped-flint wall, be prepared to pay a high price for the craftsmanship that is
required to build one.

Brick

Brick is one of the most widely used walling materials, available in a vast range of
textures, colors, and densities. The cardinal rule when choosing it is to match it to
the brick used elsewhere, in the house or adjoining walls, or in the local
neighborhood.

Brick associates well with other boundary materials, so could be used as piers in
a rough stone wall or to frame fencing. Use it also to face less attractive materials,
such as cast concrete or blockwork, especially where a strong retaining wall is
required: the concrete provides the strength, while the brick gives the decorative
finish. In terms of cost, the price of building a brick wall is less than stone, but

owing to the small size of each module the time factor in construction is high, and this is reflected in the price.

Remember that clay is porous, so the wall will need a damp-proof course (dpc) at the bottom and a weatherproof coping at the top. Dig foundations that are sufficiently deep and twice as wide as the finished wall, first removing all topsoil, which settles, so that you are working on undisturbed ground. Dig to a depth of at least 9in/225mm; on wet or spongy soil go deeper. A wall that is two bricks thick (9in/225mm) is stronger and looks better than one that is only a single brick thick. If you must build a wall that is only a single brick thick, do not make it more than 3ft/1m high. The best coping for a 9in/225mm wall is brick on edge; a double row or "creasing" course of tiles beneath the coping is not necessary. In certain situations, detailed metal copings or copings made from neat, precast concrete strips may be appropriate.

The pattern in which brick is laid is known as the "bond," and it is this that gives the wall its strength. Flemish and English bonds are quite different, so be sure to match your bond to any other brickwork in the house or garden. Pointing has a great influence on the wall's visual impact. Deeply raked-out joints cast dark shadow lines, while flush or weathered joints produce a softer and less dramatic surface.

Above left A honeycomb brick wall with arched niche and lion's mask – illuminated here at dusk – makes a decorative internal screen in a long formal South African garden.

Above right Red, brown, and yellow clays rammed in thin layers into a wooden form to produce a "mountain and cloud" pattern. A dark-brown sand was added to the original soils, which were too heavy in clay, in order to achieve the ideal 70 percent sand, 30 percent clay mix necessary for a strong rammed earth wall. The wall is in a Kyoto garden also shown on p.87.
Designer Marc Peter Keane

Not all brick walls need be solid, and a fine screen can be built using a honeycomb bond. This single-thickness wall has gaps 3-4in/75-100mm wide that allow a view through. Such a wall also acts as a windbreak, slowing the wind down rather than stopping it dead and creating turbulence as does a solid wall.

Concrete

Concrete is a much-maligned material, yet if properly used it can make durable and handsome walls suitable for many situations and particularly for today's urban gardens, where it blends well with the clean lines of modern design. Its bland surface provides a suitable background for plants. Concrete is available in the form of solid or perforated blocks, as cinder blocks made of clinker concrete and rendered, or as wet concrete laid *in situ*.

Blocks

Concrete blocks, available in many sizes, can be perfectly smooth or have a rough, textured face. The smoother the block, the more the wall seems to recede, while a textured surface tends to draw the eye and foreshorten a space.

They lend themselves to being rendered or painted, an effective way of linking the wall with an interior color scheme, and the color chosen also affects the impression of space: a wall in a cool color seems to push the boundary back, while stronger, hotter colors make the enclosed space seem smaller. Remember that white can lighten a dark situation, but is also capable of producing an uncomfortable glare even in modest sunlight.

It is much quicker to build a wall from concrete blocks than from bricks, so if you are having a wall built professionally this is a cost-cutting factor to take into account. Also, area for area, concrete is cheaper than brick. Most people think of building a concrete block wall using just one modular size, say 9x9x18in (225x225x450mm), but if you vary this by using some blocks of 9x4$\frac{1}{2}$x18in (225x112x450mm), you can set up a fascinating visual dialogue on the wall face.

Screen blocks, available in a wide range of openwork designs, are a more quickly (and cheaply) constructed alternative to plain concrete blocks, but they offer only minimal privacy and look uncomfortable in most design situations.

Cast or *in situ* concrete

This is a universally used, handsome, and widely respected material that associates well with contemporary architecture. It is the natural choice where a similar material has been used for the house. It can be cast into virtually any shape or pattern and may be given a surface finish by the "formwork" that contains it during setting. Planed lumber forms create a smooth surface, while rough-sawn lumber imparts all the intricacies of the grain, producing a remarkably subtle result. Yet another finish can be obtained by using power tools to expose the aggregate or small stones in the concrete mix once the form is removed.

Opposite Rendered concrete can produce an extremely handsome wall, particularly when color washed and etched into stone-sized blocks, as in this Sydney garden. This is a clean and elegant treatment with a strongly architectural feel.
Designer Michael Love

Below Splattering or spraying stone paint on brick or concrete walls produces a heavily textured and weatherproof finish. It can transform an ugly wall or give an old one a new lease on life. The subdued color provides a good foil for the lush planting and works well in the warm South African climate.
Designer Ray Hudson

Above left Slats set on the diagonal produce a more interesting visual rhythm than the standard horizontal or vertical approach. They have the effect of leading the eyes up or down, so remember that any plants below will become a real focus. The fence post should have been cut off with the top of the run for better effect.
Design Merrist Wood Horticultural College

Above right Slats set at right angles to one another and contained within a solid, well-detailed frame make an elegant screen in this New York roof garden. The theme is continued at a lower level on the facing of raised beds.
Designer Tim du Val

Wood

In many gardens, wooden fences are the obvious choice for the boundaries. They may be open to embrace a view or closed to maintain privacy. They offer a cheaper alternative to stone, brick, or concrete, can be constructed more quickly, and provide almost unlimited design opportunities. In a sloping garden that is in an informal or rural situation, run the fence with the lie of the land: step it up or down in sections if a strong architectural look is required. If the fence runs alongside a border, a stepping-stone path next to it makes maintenance and access to the back of the border easier.

To grow vines against the fence, screw eyes or drive nails into the supporting posts and thread horizontal wires along its length.

Panels and boards

Interwoven wooden strips made up into panels or vertical feather-edged boards, nailed onto horizontal rails, set between posts form a neutral background for planting and offer complete privacy. Panels are normally 6ft/1.8m wide and in heights up to 6ft/1.8m. Set them between wooden posts concreted into position or slotted into metal spikes driven into the ground. When using interwoven panels, make sure that the pattern of interweaving runs continuously throughout the fence. Because vertical boards taper slightly, they set up a shadow pattern and should be fitted in the same direction to maintain this pattern. Treat all plain wood with a nontoxic wood preservative that also helps to darken it when new.

Ranch fences, often seen surrounding new properties, are essentially a contemporary boundary in urban settings and should be part of an equally contemporary design. Horizontal boards about 6in/150mm wide with slight gaps between them are fitted to support posts on one side only or fitted alternately to the back and front of the run. This is called "hit-and-miss" fencing and offers slightly more privacy. Either approach produces a strong horizontal line that can be used to extend the presence of a building out into the garden: such a fence should never be angled away from the horizontal to match a slope.

Most ranch fences are painted white or stained brown (which is easier to maintain and looks better in the landscape). If you wanted to link the fence with a color used on the outside of the house, you could treat it with a nontoxic stain in one of a wide range of colors.

Slats

A slatted fence can provide an elegant boundary, and there are many different variations to choose from. The simplest are made of vertical 4-6in/100-150mm wide slats, but the use of differing widths, heights, and angles can set up all kinds of rhythmical possibilities. An interesting effect is achieved by setting them at a 45-degree angle, for example, with runs at right angles to one another in a herringbone pattern.

Screens made from vertical slats provide the perfect opportunity to continue the line and construction of a vertically boarded fence into the internal space of a

Above left A fine cedar wood fence – note how precisely the slats match on either side of the posts – makes the perfect backdrop for a profusion of pennisetum. Such a boundary is not cheap, but it will last for many years provided that it is treated regularly with nontoxic preservative.
Landscape Architects: Wolfgang Oehme and James Anthony van Sweden

Above right Simple sun-bleached boards at Stonecrop, Frank Cabot's garden in New York State, provide a stout screen and lead the eyes up toward the leafy canopy. Slight gaps between the boards visually lighten the structure, which is the perfect host for sprawling vines. The arch leads into a second room, where a further doorway heightens the distant view.

Above left Lifted out of the ordinary by a simple circular medallion, this trellis with its water feature and rampant *Mandevilla* x *amabilis* "Alice du Pont" becomes a work of art.
Designer Keith Corlett

Above right A long, robust trellis smothered with "New Dawn" roses borders the gravel path leading down to the sea at Martha's Vineyard. It is punctuated by a small arbor, the floor of which is neatly decked and set slightly higher than ground level for emphasis. Simple wooden chairs echo the color of the larger beams on the trellis.
Designer Edwina von Gal

garden. They can simply be set at a right angle to the main fence, or tailored to a curve by bolting each slat to a metal arris rail that in turn is set between wooden or metal posts. Vary the height of the screen to direct the eye, perhaps down to a tension point, or use it to partially enclose a feature, such as a pool or statue, thus enhancing its qualities as a focal point.

Trellis

Trellis made of laths of lumber is one of the most successful screening materials, providing an excellent framework for climbing plants and a useful way of subdividing a garden. Standard panels, up to 6ft/1.8m square, are sold in garden centers, but it is a relatively easy matter to make your own, to your own design and dimensions. In a small garden use the simplest type: larger plots may be enhanced by more ornate trelliswork, possibly used in conjunction with a formal floor pattern and formalized planting to create a focal point. The more ornate trelliswork also lends itself to painting, usually in the blue/gray color range, but remember that the stronger the background color, the more it will impinge on the color scheme of the planting.

Pickets, palings, and hurdles

Where privacy is not a factor, such as at the front of a house, a picket fence may be a good choice. Traditionally these simple slatted fences with pointed tops are painted white, though a more modern treatment uses rounded tops, and in certain

parts of North America very elaborate designs are to be found.

For a low, unobtrusive but stockproof fence in an informal situation such as a semiwild or woodland area, choose chestnut palings. Usually about 3ft/1m high, the cleft chestnut pales are spaced approximately 4in/100mm apart and are tied to one another by galvanized wire. Runs are sold in rolls and can be stapled to round posts driven firmly into the ground.

An excellent temporary screen in a rural situation can be created with hurdle fencing made from woven strips of hazel and originally used for penning sheep. Each hurdle measures 6ft/1.8m square and in a domestic situation is wired to round supporting posts. Their lifespan of 8-10 years is relatively short, but they make a useful barrier while a hedge or other boundary-forming planting is growing. Osier hurdles, made from strips of willow, can be used in the same way.

Post-and-rail fences

The simple post-and-rail fence, which is often used to surround paddocks, and which consists of two, three, or sometimes four cleft rails mortised into posts, is strong enough to be stockproof but may be visually intrusive if it is set against rising ground or a fine view, or, even worse, if it is painted white. To counteract this, position the fence just behind a slightly contoured area or in a dip. In order to make post-and-rail fences child- or pet-proof, add a lower section of squared galvanized "sheep" wire.

Above Picket fences are universally popular, particularly for front gardens, which are intended to be on show. There are numerous variations in style, and here the posts, which are carried slightly higher than the main run, have been thoughtfully finished. Using pickets at a lower level to define the borders introduces a note of control amid exuberant planting. A solid boundary would not have worked in this situation, since it would have divorced the wonderful backdrop of trees from the intimate area close to the house.
Designers Peter Wooster, Gary Keim

Metal

Whether wrought or cast iron or aluminum, metal fences are expensive but are the perfect choice in a situation where maintaining a view is important. Park railings, traditionally about 4ft/1.5m high and with two or three black-painted rails, merge particularly well into the landscape. In an urban street, post-and-chain fences, which offer no privacy and little in the way of a physical boundary, can provide demarcation for a front garden. The traditional pattern uses wooden or stone posts approximately 2½ ft/750mm high with black-painted chains of cast iron (never plastic) hung in gentle loops between them. It is best to use this type of fence to match that of neighboring houses.

Cast iron

Railings of cast iron were traditionally used either in urban situations or to form a boundary around fine country houses. Their often delicate patterns form a tracery, which can be an excellent foil for both architecture and planting. Be sure to choose simple designs and stick to a generous-grade gauge of metal.

Chain link

Chain link and its derivatives make high-security fences. With their plastic-coated posts and wire, chain-link fences are long lasting, and a black or brown coating (unlike a green one) blends well into the landscape. In a situation where they can be softened by vines, these fences become virtually invisible.

Below In this garden in London, England, low iron railings establish a boundary. Painted black, they allow the view to run through with minimal disruption, thus increasing the feeling of spaciousness. White would reflect the light and be visually uncomfortable and surprisingly difficult to look through. Pointed finials provide a decorative touch and, even on a fence of this height, a useful deterrent.

Glass

Clear glass screens (wired for safety) set in a wooden or aluminum frame will act as a windbreak in a garden where strong winds are a problem but the view is worth preserving. Set the edges of the frame so that they do not block your view whether you are sitting or standing.

When planning a sunroom or greenhouse extension, consider it as one of your outdoor rooms and, matching its design with that of the house, make sure it also works with the style of the garden.

New directions

On the cutting edge of garden design are "walls" made from woven polyester, which is light, rot-resistant, and translucent, so it does not cast a shadow on the garden. It comes in rolls of virtually any width, which you can stretch and attach to lightweight aluminum frames bolted to alloy posts. The whole of a run, including posts, is a fraction of the weight of other types of fencing.

Plastics of all kinds are another option: they are colorful and can be molded to different shapes, patterns, and curves. Fiber optics offer further possibilities. They could be woven into a hazel or willow hurdle fence or through the branches of a hedge to add drama and sparkle.

Above The yew topiary at Little Malvern Court in Herefordshire, England was planted in the early years of this century by the present owner's grandfather. A massive and glorious example of the art, as well as a stock-proof evergreen barrier, it has no particular symbolism, simply reflecting a love of eccentric shapes.

Right The small leaves of this well-tended escallonia hedge help create a feeling of greater space; bold foliage would have the opposite effect. Because it is kept well-trimmed, this hedge, in Christchurch, New Zealand, never flowers. The eyes are drawn along both hedges to the sculptural focal point.
Designer Robert Watson

Living materials

Vegetative "walls" can be used on their own or in combination with material walls or fences. As well as hedges for boundaries, plants may be used to form internal divisions without creating a physical barrier or to define the edges of paved or planted areas.

Hedges

A hedge is relatively cheap, long-lasting, and can provide changing foliage throughout the year. In an exposed situation it provides excellent shelter, filtering the wind through its branches, while in an urban location its dense foliage helps to reduce noise. You can shape a formal hedge to virtually any pattern, trimming or scalloping it to create emphasis or tension and thus making a definite design point. For an informal situation, a boundary of *Rosa rugosa* blends with a rural setting, forms a virtually impenetrable hedge, and has the benefit of flowers, foliage, and colorful hips. An in-between alternative is a tapestry hedge of mostly evergreens (boxwood with holly for example) that provides year-round color and interest, and in a rural situation a rich habitat for a wide range of wildlife and plants.

Hedges, of course, make good internal screens and provide the perfect link with hedge boundaries. They can be trimmed and swooped, trained and topiaried, or simply planted to break a sight line. Compact low-growing hedges provide effective outlines and can make a strong enough statement to indicate the

perimeters of an outdoor room. Dwarf boxwood and holly, ground-cover roses, hardy hebes, and sweet-smelling lavender are among a multitude of woody plants that can be sheared to create tidy horizontal demarcation lines.

On the debit side, hedges take time to get established and need regular maintenance in the form of trimming and fertilizing. Choose the species you plant carefully, because different types of hedging offer different characteristics. For example, a fast-growing hedge needs more trimming, while a slow-growing one will take time to reach the height you require. Avoid fast-growing varieties unless you wish to screen a particularly bad view at a high level that would be expensive or structurally impossible to disguise with a high wall.

Whatever plants you choose, thorough soil preparation is vital. Excavate a trench at least 1ft/300mm deep, and use good quality topsoil mixed with a slow-release fertilizer and plenty of organic material such as well-rotted manure or compost.

CHOOSING A HEDGE

Evergreen

Name	Height/Zone		Growth rate/Pruning	Other characteristics
Buxus sempervirens (Boxwood) *B.s.* 'Suffruticosa'	6in–8ft/15cm– 2.5m	Z6	Slow. Shape 3–4 times during growing season. Withstands hard pruning. Minimal pruning.	Ideal for formal hedge and topiary. Dwarf form for low edging, knot gardens, etc.
Caragena arborescens	to 7ft/ 2m	Z2	Fast. May be clipped or unclipped.	Highly tolerant. Makes good windbreak. Yellow flowers.
Choisya ternata (Mexican orange blossom)	3–7ft/ 1–2m	Z8	Fast. For best informal effect, do not prune.	Good informal hedge. Glassy green leaves and fragrant white flowers in spring.
Cupressus sempervirens (Italian cypress)	to 50ft/ 15m	Z8–9	Fast growing when young. No pruning necessary.	Aromatic gray/green foliage. Suitable for a Mediterranean-type climate.
Escallonia	4–6ft/1.2– 1.8m	Z7–9	Moderate to fast. Clip after flowering or leave to form high, loose hedge.	White, red or pink flowers. Suitable for coastal gardens.
Ilex aquifolium (English holly)	7–12ft/ 2–4m	Z7	Slow-growing. Prune once in midsummer.	White flowers and red berries on female plants if male plants nearby. Excellent dense, prickly hedge.
Lavandula (Lavender)	12–24in/ 30–60cm	Z6	Moderate. Clip in spring or after flowering for neat appearance.	Gray, aromatic foliage, purple flowers. Low-growing, ideal for edging.
Lonicera nitida	20in–7ft/ 50cm–2m	Z7	Fast. Clip regularly to prevent legginess. Prune hard in early spring to stimulate growth.	Good hedging material.
Prunus laurocerasus (Cherry laurel, laurel)	7–16ft/ 2–5m	Z7	Slow. Prune carefully once a year in early summer rather than clip.	Makes a fine dense hedge.
Rosmarinus officinalis (Rosemary)	to 5ft/ 1.5m	Z8	Fast. Clip often when young to encourage bushiness.	Aromatic. Used as a herb. Suitable for a Mediterranean-type climate.

Name	Height/Zone		Growth rate/Pruning	Other characteristics
Santolina chamaecyparissus (Cotton lavender)	to 30in/ 75cm	Z7	Moderate. Clip immediately after flowering, if flowers are required, otherwise in spring.	Low-growing, aromatic gray foliage and yellow button flowers mid to late summer.
Taxus baccata (Yew)	5–12ft/ 1.5–4m	Z6	Moderate. Prune once in late summer. Can be clipped to any shape.	Possibly the finest hedge. Dark green poisonous leaves and poisonous berries.
Taxus cuspidata (Japanese yew)	to 33ft/ 10m	Z4	As *T. baccata*.	Spreading habit. Dark green leaves. Suitable for cold winter climates.
Tsuga canadensis (Canada hemlock)	to 50ft/ 15m	Z3	Fast. Can be kept clipped or unclipped.	One of the best conifers for cold winter climates. Good windbreak.

Deciduous

Name	Height/Zone		Growth rate/Pruning	Other characteristics
Berberis thunbergii	3–6ft/ 1–1.8m	Z5	Moderate. Trim once in summer.	Makes a dense, spiny hedge of small, bright green leaves. Good fall color.
Carpinus betulus (Common hornbeam)	5–10ft/ 1.5–3m	Z5	Moderate. Trim once during growing season.	Makes a fine hedge. Similar to *Fagus sylvatica* but can grow in heavy, damp soil.
Cornus alba (Red-barked dogwood)	to 10ft/ 3m	Z2	Fast. Cut back in spring every other year.	Makes good informal hedge. Young stems red in winter.
Fagus sylvatica (European beech)	5–10ft/ 1.5–3m	Z4	Moderate. Trim once during growing season.	Russet-brown fall leaves are held throughout winter.
Potentilla fruticosa	to 5ft/ 1.5m	Z3	Moderate. Prune early spring to control growth.	An excellent informal hedge with yellow flowers throughout summer.
Rosa rugosa (Hedgehog rose)	30in–3ft/ 75cm–1m	Z2	Moderate. Prune once in summer and once in dormant period.	Repeat-flowering. Forms a good informal hedge. Suitable for cold winter climates.

Trees

Trees that respond to training and shearing can be interlaced to make interesting raised screens for boundaries or to define a drive, walk, or pathway (shrubs trained as standards can perform a similar function). A line of trees is allowed to grow to a given height, then the tops are pollarded or trained and sheared into a continuous block to form a high-level "hedge" with a row of clean, bare trunks below. A screen composed of interlaced trees or shrubs can give an impressive sense of scale and strength of purpose to a garden. Although the trunks are all that obstruct the view at ground level, the sense of containment is remarkably strong. These hedges on stilts need precise training and cutting, at a high level.

Espaliered fruit trees can be planted at regular intervals along a wall to add interest or trained along wires as freestanding screens. Traditional in old walled gardens, trained trees are just as valuable in modern small plots for creating space-saving divisions (and providing fruit crops) and the low-growing "step-over" varieties can be planted to make attractive low-level "edgings."

Fedge

A "fedge" is a cross between a fence and a hedge. The framework is wire or plastic mesh stretched between posts or attached to a simple trellis. Train a fast-growing vine, such as ivy or honeysuckle, over it. This will form a green wall or screen far quicker than a hedge and can easily be kept in shape by pruning or shearing. Rope swags between wooden posts or stone or brick pillars can form a host for climbing plants to make attractive internal screens.

Above Interlaced Japanese katsuras (cercidiphyllums) integrated into this composition at the bottom of the slope balance the dominant bulk of the house at the top. This is an excellent example of the asymmetric planning I describe on p.46. The plants cascade down between lines of railroad ties like waves breaking on a seashore.
Designer Barbara Thomas

Opposite A low, meandering, softly rounded boxwood hedge defines an inviting garden room and divides a generous softly planted border. A rigid angular shape would not have worked as well in this informal setting.

81

ENTRANCES AND TRANSITION POINTS

First impressions, whether at the entrance to the garden or at the transition point from one outdoor room to another, anticipate what lies beyond and make important punctuating statements within the overall design. An opening in a wall or hedge need not be filled at all, the glimpse through being enough to draw the eye to pleasures beyond the gap. If you decide to fill it with a gate or door or to frame it with an arch, consider not only the material (and base your choice on one that links with the "wall" into which it is set) but also the proportions. A tall narrow opening is less inviting than a wide one.

Doors and gates

Gates can be either solid, maintaining privacy, or they may allow a sight of the view beyond. They can serve either pedestrians or vehicles, though the two are often combined, particularly in small gardens, with one section opening for people, two together for cars. Make sure a gate is wide enough for the purpose for

Above A minimal framework of iron hoops clad with climbing roses marks the transition point between two garden rooms at Manor Farm near Bath, England.

Below left The solidity of this door is positive yet inviting. Impeccably detailed, it is very much a part of the wall. What lies beyond it? A secret garden, perhaps? The mood is slightly mysterious, the end result private.

Below right A fine wrought-iron gate allows an enticing glimpse of the garden room on the other side. It aligns with an opening in the yew hedge beyond which is another garden room, with a lily pool.

which it is intended; if it matches the height of the boundary either side, it will look most comfortable. Take advantage of the opportunity to create interesting and attractive counterpoints: a finely detailed wrought-iron gate in a brick or stone wall, or a simply worked wooden gate in a hedge can look superb.

Arches

Arches, too, can become punctuation marks within a design, while acting as a transitional element between different areas. They concentrate a view, or direct feet and eyes to a specific point, creating tension for a moment, then releasing it. Use them to offer low-key support for vines, emphasizing the fact that the plants are the real stars of the garden. Hedges can be trained to form living arches; they may be woven from willow or even interlaced from hornbeam or linden. Arches can be constructed from brick, stone, wood, or metal. The most important thing to remember, as always, is that they should respect and blend with the overall style and materials used elsewhere in the garden.

Below left Imposing yet elegant, this gate has enormous physical strength but still allows a partial view through when closed. Traditional designs such as this are costly to reproduce today, though in the right situation they are worth it.

Below right Highly individualistic wood arches, in harmony with the wood-built house, set up a strong feeling of movement emphasized by the narrow brick path. Such powerful architecture must clearly fit into an overall plan if it is to succeed.

Above This is an effective and simple way to pierce a boundary, and it introduces both light and lightness to a shady corner of the garden. The gravel path and edging are equally restrained, allowing the planting to steal the show.

Above A double row of white birches creates a translucent, leafy ceiling with a constant play of light and shadow. The quality and amount of light filtering down through leaves, and the mood it creates, depends on the species of tree. With white birch, it is never too heavy and even in winter the delicate tracery of branches forms a lofty lattice against the sky.

Opposite A leafy ceiling is created next to the house by growing a grapevine on overhead beams. These form a link with the building, extending its line out into the garden. Here rounded wooden poles echo the shape of the white columns and act as host to the grapevine, roses, and ivy.

THE CEILING

Many people are so preoccupied with other facets of the garden and planting that they forget the important vertical space above. If you walk through woodland, the comforting feeling of enclosure is heightened by the overhead canopy of branches that creates the dappled shadows and provides shelter from wind. In a garden open to the vast canopy of the sky, that intimacy is lost.

When planning the garden, then, consider the possibilities of making tunnels and pergola walks as corridors, or using overhead beams and awnings to make ceilings over open sitting areas, and of planting trees and tall shrubs to make leafy canopies. Keep the design simple, bearing in mind that features used close to the house, such as overhead beams, can be more formal and architectural, while in farther parts of the garden, arbors and tunnels will come into their own. Ceilings can be functional, too: the leafy canopy formed by two sturdy trees could create a pleasantly shaded spot for a hammock; a wooden frame for a swing might be converted later into an arch for a climbing rose or be extended into a pergola.

As you plan, you will realize that an outdoor "ceiling" has a huge advantage over an indoor one, for it can be enhanced by a host of climbing plants that blend into a soft canopy. Even in winter it will contribute to your outdoor room by casting interesting shadows on the floor.

Canopies, tunnels, and corridors

An orchard or area of woodland, even a single tree with a spreading canopy, can bring a feeling of intimacy and peace to the garden, as well as offering shade and shelter. Trees and shrubs with overhanging branches form natural tunnels along a path and throw the brightness of open glades into starker contrast. For a more controlled tunnel, provide a frame over the path on which to train plants such as laburnums, wisteria, grapevines, roses, or fruit trees.

Like leafy tunnels, freestanding pergolas are garden corridors or colonnades that link two areas or frame a path. Straight pergolas can be used as a single run or set at right angles to each other to form a cross-axis within the overall garden pattern. Entering a curved pergola will engender a feeling of mystery and emerging from the far end, a sense of a release of tension.

A statue or urn placed at the end of a pergola draws the eye and foreshortens the space. If you wish to avoid this, either soften the terminal views with planting or align the pergola so that it embraces a vista that slowly unfolds as you walk along. The construction of the path beneath the pergola will also determine the speed at which you walk through it (see p.88).

As a general rule, the larger the garden, the more massive the pergola's construction can be. In a spacious setting, use stone or brick piers that take their cue from materials used elsewhere in the garden, with cross-beams of generously

Above Trees set in a lawn cast shadow patterns that set up visual divisions on the grass below – patterns that change constantly as they swing across the area in the course of the day. As well as offering much-needed shade, in bright light climates such patterns are exploited as a design tool. This approach is equally successful in the softer light of a temperate climate.

Right The lightness of the canopy is appropriate, gently focusing rather than detracting from the view in this Connecticut garden.

Canvas canopies and awnings can filter sunlight, providing an altogether softer feel than overheads. They can be folded away when not in use and taken down for cleaning.
Designer John Saladino

sectioned lumber and the path wide beneath. You have only to look at pergolas in gardens designed by Lutyens – Hestercombe in Somerset, England being a perfect example – to see a pergola used at its powerful best.

In a smaller garden, scale down the design but keep it as generous as possible. Sawn lengths of lumber look better and last longer than rustic bark-covered poles. Plastic-covered metal hoops and arches linked longitudinally by spars of the same material are easy to erect but can lack visual power, although those made in bright, primary colors can look wonderful in a modern situation.

Overheads

Beams adjoining a building and extending over a sitting area or passageway act as a strong element linking house and garden. They help to define a space, the latticed ceiling bringing intimacy to an otherwise open area, and perhaps with vines casting light shade. For denser shade in sunny climates, set the beams at an angle and "roof" them over with tiles or combine the construction with a fabric awning that can be rolled away. Consider using overheads or an awning to provide screening from high-level windows in neighboring properties. In an urban situation where high walls surround a yard or basement, they fulfill a similar role to a false ceiling in a room with too much height. If you paint the walls beneath overhead beams in a pale color, this will also help to define the space, reflect the light, and add to the feeling of intimacy.

Overhead beams extending over a passageway provide an arcade or walkway and distract the attention from the high walls on either side.

Above left Overheads are part of a successfully integrated approach to the design of a New York roof garden. In exposed situations such as this, screens are needed not only from neighboring roofs and windows but also from sun and, possibly, gusty winds. Plants, therefore, need to be robust.
Designer Keith Corlett

Above right The symmetry of the bamboo ceiling in the garden of a Samurai house in Kyoto (see also p.69) contrasts with the informal but carefully chosen planting below. The screen is one of several in this garden, where their role is both aesthetic and functional.
Designer Marc Peter Keane

Above The garden floor often forms a natural progression from the floor inside the house. Depending on how you treat it, it may lead and draw the eye out into the garden, produce a static pattern, or simply form a neutral background. Here, parallel courses of basketweave brick draw the eye to the deck that is turned at right angles to slow the view down. Gravel provides punctuation before leading onto the broad lawn. Two closely planted cypresses heighten the drama, providing a powerful visual magnet.

THE FLOOR

The garden's horizontal surface – its "floor" – is one of the most important elements in terms of visual impact, practicality, and cost. It will almost certainly be made from both hard and soft landscape materials – grass and other carpeting plants. In a well-designed ground plan, the hard landscape provides a subtle combination of paved areas, paths, drives, and parking areas. These should never dominate but rather should form the underlying structure of the composition.

The paths that link the various elements of your composition – terrace, lawn, greenhouse, play area, and so on – can also serve an aesthetic purpose, leading both feet and eyes in the direction of a garden feature, or stopping to pause at a seat or restful view. Make them sufficiently wide, ideally a minimum of 2ft/600mm, to allow not just for feet, but also for wheelbarrows and children's toys.

The characteristics of different floor materials and how they are laid have a real impact on the end result and on cost. Large slabs of natural stone or precast concrete are ideal for terraces and paths with straight sides; to fit a curve, they need cutting, which is skilled, expensive, and time-consuming; an alternative is to fill the gaps between the slabs with small cobbles bedded flush with the surface or leave them open and fill with topsoil and aromatic, low-growing plants. Smaller modules such as bricks, Belgian blocks, or cobbles conform much more easily to a curve; although expensive, they are simpler and cheaper to lay in an intricate pattern. Fluid surfaces such as gravel, stone chips, or concrete can be cast or laid to flowing curves with minimal effort and maximum effect. Grass paths provide soft links, especially appropriate between lawned areas; if subject to heavy use, set stepping stones at a slightly lower level than the grass to take the wear and tear.

The shape and size of a particular slab or module affects the overall impression of space. A terrace or drive laid with large panels of exposed aggregate concrete will seem far larger than one laid with bricks or small concrete blocks. The "busy" pattern encourages the eye to dwell on it longer and in more detail, while large, unobstructed panels draw the eye onward and outward. A pattern with many conflicting lines and angles, such as random paving, looks uncomfortable in a clean, crisp architectural situation close to a house and is better used in a more distant and informal part of the garden. Long narrow modules laid in a staggered bond across a terrace make it seem wider, while square slabs in a plain grid are more formal and controlled. Bricks laid across a path will be visually more static than bricks laid down its length. Heighten the effect further by emphasizing the crosswise joints or pointing, or by raking them out to create a shadow line. This is an effective design tool and provides a particularly architectural treatment.

Surface texture plays its part too. Lay a smooth, polished area to give the impression of size and to encourage fast movement, but a textured surface to slow down both eyes and feet. The practicalities of laying a horizontal surface also have to be taken into account, particularly where it adjoins the house, and it must be laid so that it sheds rainwater. This means constructing it at least 6in/150mm below the damp-proof course and with a slight slope or fall away from the building toward a planted area or drain. Foundations are essential, and the better the preparation the more durable the end result. Bed any paved surface on mortar over a consolidated layer of rubble or crushed stone 4in/100mm thick. There are some possible variations, particularly with certain kinds of bricks or blocks that form a "flexible sidewalk." These are normally bedded on sand and are contained within a restraining edge that holds the whole surface together. For bricks, brush a dry mortar mix into the joints and water carefully; for blocks, sand is normally used and the whole surface consolidated with a flat-plate vibrator.

Manholes and drains seem invariably to be in the most difficult position, right in the middle of a terrace and almost always set at an awkward angle to the house. If this angle is not too acute, manhole covers and the frames into which they fit can often be lifted and reset at a right angle to the building or, if they are situated in the middle of paving, they can be reset at an angle that blends with the angles of the paving joints. An alternative is to buy a recessed cover into which paving can be set so that the manhole blends into the overall surface. A further alternative is to try and work the manhole into a planted area, perhaps covering it with smooth boulders and loose cobbles that can be removed for access.

Drains pose another problem, since they are usually close to the house. Try, when planning any paved area, to make them unobtrusive. If possible, position them at the junction of two intersecting courses of brick or paving, or at the center of a radiating pattern, where they will become part of the floorscape.

Below In my own gardens I aim for an integrated blend of hard and soft landscape to form a balanced composition. The floor clearly plays a major structural role in binding the various elements of the garden together, and here I have used a combination of mellow brick, old York stone, and gravel. The latter provides an ideal foil for the planting, which has been kept within the pastel color range, with just a dash of strong yellow. Brick walls, in harmony with those used on the floor, and wrought-iron gates mark the boundary between this and the next garden room, where a stone urn, simply planted with a single color, provides a strong focal point.

Natural Stone

There are many different kinds of natural stone for paving. Color, density, and cost all vary, but in general this is the most expensive type of paving. Among its subtle beauties are slight variations in surface texture and color; manufactured slabs with rough surfaces successfully reproduce these textural qualities, but color variations cannot be captured.

Slabs

Sandstones of varying types are the most common, and Tennessee fieldstone is typical and widely used in North America. Secondhand random rectangular slabs that were originally used as sidewalk or factory flooring can be found, but it is important to check the source, because the latter may be impregnated with oil that can "sweat" out in hot weather and be carried indoors. The thickness varies from 2-4in/50-100mm, and this means a corresponding variation in the level of the foundation on which it is laid.

Lay stone paving carefully, with the slabs radiating out from a central "key stone." Stagger the joints as much as possible to ensure that there are never more than three joints running together in a continuous line. Either point the joints neatly and rub them slightly back, or rake them right out and fill them with soil sown with alpine or other low-growing plants. You can leave out the occasional

Above Hard landscaping need not be strictly architectural, and this sinuous sweep of Pennsylvania blue-stone slabs is aligned with great drifts of ornamental grasses. Such a path flows like a stream between the grassy areas – the open joints colonized by mazus only adding to the informality of the composition.
Landscape Architects: Wolfgang Oehme and James Anthony van Sweden

Right Large slabs of natural stone are often heavy enough to be bedded on sifted soil, although there will often be, as here, some slight settlement. Laying slabs in this way allows plants to self-seed or to be intentionally sown in crevices, adding to the feeling of informality.

small slab and either plant the space or fill it with a contrasting material such as bricks or small cobbles.

Slate

Slate is a dramatically dark stone, usually with a smooth polished finish that is almost black when wet and that can get alarmingly hot underfoot in the sun. Unlike many other natural stones, slate is ideal for paving inside the house as well as outside. Lay it using the same bond and following the same direction to provide the perfect link between the two areas. Its color makes it useful as a contrast with the paler surfaces of chippings or of light foliage such as the gray leaves of *Senecio* "Sunshine," artemisia, or the steel-blue of *Festuca glauca*.

Granite

Granite is another expensive, high-class paving. In its polished form, it best suits high-tech, contemporary situations, but Belgian blocks, traditionally used as street paving, are less expensive. Blocks are approximately the size of a brick; they are also available in a half size, roughly 4in/100mm square. You can sometimes find granite paving in larger sizes at demolition yards. It looks superb when laid next to a house built from a similar material.

Granite's slightly uneven surface makes it ideal where grip is important, as on a sloping path or driveway, but is perhaps a less obvious choice for a terrace or patio,

Above Irregular materials, such as broken or random paving, have an inherently busy outline, but can be successfully incorporated into a terrace if contained within panels, in this case fine pieces of sawn stone. The same blue stone is used as a seat around the raised pool, overhanging the random stone wall to cast a deep shadow. *Landscape Architects: Wolfgang Oehme and James Anthony van Sweden*

Left Slate can be very variable in color, which gives it character, and because it cuts easily it is ideal in architectural schemes where precision is important. Here, it is laid in a basketweave pattern to provide a finely detailed floor in a subtle range of hues.

Above Thousands of cobbles contained by courses of brick that radiate out from the raised pool are laid on end or sideways in alternating segments. The circular pool is emphasized by the low, carefully trimmed hedge and a band of bricks. Carefully positioned terra-cotta pots, some with boxwood spheres, provide punctuation and add weight to the central feature.

Magical in its effect, this design shows a deep understanding of the materials used and is based on a strong yet simple concept – as are all successful designs.

Designers Claus Scheinert, Tom Parr

where you may wish to stand tables and chairs. Belgian blocks make an excellent edge to a gravel drive, where they can be firmly set in concrete.

Marble

At its best this is a classy, glitzy paving whose highly polished surface shimmers in the rain. Use it in its sawn rectangular form in highly stylized, architectural situations teamed with contrasting materials to set off its natural beauty.

Cobbles

These are smooth, water-washed stones of varying sizes similar to those found on beaches – from where, incidentally, it is usually illegal to remove them. Like Belgian blocks, they were once used as street paving, often in intricate patterns. In the garden, lay them as a contrast material to other paving or, in the smaller sizes, to replace small slabs in a random terrace or to fill the triangular joints of a curving slab path. Strong sweeps look good where planting is difficult to establish, such as beneath trees or in dry locations, when they should be laid loose without mortar.

Pack them together as tightly as possible, with no mortar showing between the joints, or use them loose, possibly in conjunction with larger boulders and planting. The latter treatment is virtually impossible to walk on. Used in a front garden, where callers may be tempted to take a short cut to the main entrance, it says, very firmly, "keep off."

Chippings

Chippings are simply broken stone. They come in a wide range of colors, sizes, and textures and, like cobbles, make excellent ground cover, perhaps with some sculptural planting growing through the surface. The palest shades are virtually

white and somewhat glaring in strong sunlight, but they can be ideal in a shady situation such as a basement garden or dark yard, where they reflect the light. In a shady garden with dark planting, a slate sidewalk with white chippings surrounding green malachite boulders would look stunning.

Gravel

It would be difficult to find a more versatile surface that is low in cost and equally at home in a crisp urban situation, formal parterre, or country cottage-style garden. Use it for paths or drives, but ensure that it is well laid, particularly where there is traffic over it. For best results have it laid by a professional landscape contractor, who will make a base of crushed stone or rubble, topped by chippings and a clay binder. The final, thin layer is of rounded, washed pea gravel. Each layer must be well compacted before the next is added, and paths and drives must be laid with a slight camber so they shed water to either side.

Unless gravel is allowed to run beneath or "die out" in surrounding planting, you must lay a retaining edge. As a rule, avoid the concrete curb edging supplied in yard/meter lengths. Although practical for a straight run, it looks cheap, and when set to a curve produces a series of unsightly angles. A better choice is brick, laid end to end, or Belgian blocks "haunched" or set in concrete. Other alternatives include pressure-treated lumber boards pegged firmly in position. Cast-iron edging strip, sometimes seen in older gardens, is expensive but superb.

Gravel can also be used in conjunction with planting, as a low-maintenance ground cover. For best results, lay it over a weak mix of concrete, leaving gaps for the plants to grow through.

Above left Gravel is one of the most attractive floor coverings: it acts as a superb foil to planting as well as other hard surfaces. Here, there is a natural progression from the formality of the basketweave paving bricks, softened by plants, through the graveled area, set about with pots and low table, to the informality of the open countryside.

Above right Large gravel stones are used to make an informal path between two borders of hardy perennials. In such a situation, the material need not be restrained and can simply die off at random into the planting on either side. The path bends away out of sight, adding an air of mystery to the composition.
Designer Christopher Grey-Wilson

Concrete

While natural materials can look wonderful, they are not necessarily the best choice in all situations. Concrete – *the* material of the twentieth century – may work far better in a contemporary setting and sometimes a combination of precast concrete with brick or a natural material gives a superb effect.

Slabs

These are widely used and available in an enormous range of shapes, sizes, colors, textures, and patterns. The best provide a good imitation of natural stone at about half the price, these usually being a neutral gray color, or with a sandy "Cotswold" finish. Clearly, where large quantities of a natural-looking stone are required, they

Above Concrete cast in large panels gives an architectural and uniform floor. Shadow patterns thrown by the wooden roofs are fascinating and offer welcome relief from the glare of the hot Californian sun.

Right Colored concrete was cast *in situ* to make bold panels of irregular size. Such a surface is elegant and hardwearing – and by comparison with other paving materials, relatively cheap. It is thus a good choice for covering large areas, though its uniformity of color and texture demands good planting to provide additional interest.
Designer Beth Chatto

make a sensible choice: their rough surface is convincing (though it makes them slightly unstable for tables and chairs), and only a trained eye would notice the absence of the subtle color variations present in natural stone. Lay concrete slabs as described on p.90.

Precast slabs designed to imitate other surfaces, such as bricks or Belgian blocks, are somewhat less convincing. If you cannot afford the real thing, rather than opt for a poor imitation it is better to choose something quite different with no pretensions to being other than itself. Plain, smooth, precast concrete comes in rectangular, square, and circular slabs as well as in hexagons and other less usual shapes. Some of these shapes may produce a visually busy pattern if used over a substantial area, but you might consider using hexagons, for example, as a path through an informal area of planting. They work especially well if you stagger the edge of the path so that it "dies off" into the foliage on either side.

Blocks

Concrete paving blocks, in various colors including brown, gray, and pink, were widely used for drives and parking areas until the introduction of extremely durable paving bricks, when their popularity declined. However, though slightly smaller than bricks (they measure 4x8 in/100x200mm), because they are cheaper, they may still be an attractive proposition for covering a large area. They can be laid easily and speedily over sharp sand on a layer of well-compacted rubble, and can easily be lifted if necessary. They need an edge restraint, usually special blocks set in concrete, although a board edging might also be used. This kind of "flexible sidewalk" sinks slightly beneath heavy traffic but then springs back to its original profile.

Cast concrete

Cast or *in situ* concrete can be poured to virtually any shape and can be given special finishes before it sets. Eliminating the cutting necessary for slabs makes it cost-effective and straightforward to lay. A long straightedge tamped over a path or parking area will produce a ribbed effect, while a steel float gives a polished and a wooden float a slightly textured result.

"Impressed" concrete, usually laid by specialists, is a direct imitation of other surfaces, and in my opinion visually dishonest. The concrete has a dye incorporated into it and is then pressed with molds to create any finish from fake cobbles to natural stone.

A particularly attractive finish is achieved by exposing the aggregate or small stones in a concrete mix by brushing or spraying with water just before the surface finally sets. The effect varies according to the aggregate. Another technique is to "seed" the wet concrete with the aggregate, then carefully tamp it in – a finish that resembles a gravel path or drive with the surface firmly held in position.

Since large areas of concrete are subject to expansion and contraction, panels are

Above I used a combination of brick and old York stone on the terrace next to the house and precast concrete slabs set in the lawn to form a stepping-stone path. It sweeps around carefully molded contours, pausing at the white seat before disappearing behind the wings of planting and leading to a hidden swimming pool.

Below Concrete can be pressed into blocks, not unlike Belgian blocks in shape but lacking their natural irregularity and color variation. They are, however, much cheaper and can be ideal for drives and parking areas. *Design Berry's Garden Co.*

Right Panels of seeded aggregate are perfect around this pool, offering a firm grip when wet and an interesting surface texture. The panels are framed by narrow expansion joints – an integral part of the overall pattern, linking with the adjoining slate steps and the pool surround.
Landscape Architects: Wolfgang Oehme and James Anthony van Sweden

Below Terra-cotta tiles make a warmly textured floor in a tiny, frost-free yard in London, England, where visual interest centers on the shaped trellis and water feature.
Designer Judith Sharpe

usually poured in rectangles no more than 12ft/4m square and are laid with expansion joints between each panel. The joints can be treated as part of the overall design, constructed from brick, other types of paving, or wooden strips.

Tiles

Tiles are another small-scale paving material that form a perfect link between house and garden. They are available in many shapes, colors, and textures ranging from natural unglazed terra-cotta to brightly patterned glazed tiles. As a general rule, choose plain, mellow terra-cotta to blend with natural garden colors. Brightly colored glazed tiles can be tempting, particularly as they are easy to keep clean – though slippery when wet – but they really only look good in strongly sunlit Mediterranean settings, where the bright sun tones down any stridency. Since tiles are difficult to cut, it is best to use them for areas with long, straight sides rather than complicated curves.

If you live in an area where severe frosts are a possibility, make sure that the tiles you buy are frost-proof, checking with the manufacturers if necessary. To ensure a good surface, set them in a continuous layer of mortar on top of well-compacted rubble. Handmade tiles will need fairly wide gaps between them to allow for any unevenness in size, but other tiles can be set close together and finished with neat pointing.

Brick

Brick makes a fine and versatile paving material: it may be warm in color and texture or, in the case of some engineering bricks, crisply dark and austere. Use bricks in combination with natural stone slabs or cobbles to frame panels of precast concrete, or as an edging to lawns or other planted areas. Or use them simply to provide a paved area in their own right. Brick provides an excellent visual link with an adjoining brick building and with other brick-built features such as walls or raised beds.

Bricks vary enormously in their density, and this affects their wearing powers and weather-resistance, so it is important to choose the correct sort. House bricks can be used, but check their durability with the supplier or manufacturer. Alternatively, choose one of the specialized paving bricks that are extremely durable and can be used in a wide variety of situations, including drives and parking areas. Because they are small, bricks take longer to lay, and this, of course, is reflected in professional labor costs.

Below left Attention to detail is the hallmark of good design. Bricks, small modules that can easily be laid to curves or angles, have been carefully cut to conform to the change in direction of a hexagonal path that swings around a rudbeckia border. *Landscape Architects: Wolfgang Oehme and James Anthony van Sweden*

Below right A corner is cut to a miter in the edging pattern of warm red brick that divides a rich border from the trimmed hedge. *Designer Arabella Lennox-Boyd*

Above left Herringbone brick paving forms a traditional but busy pattern that works well in an outdoor room of this size. A single flooring material gives an area great visual strength and continuity, but care must be taken to prevent its being overpowering.

Above right Paving bricks, laid in a basketweave pattern, provide a crisp, good-looking, low-maintenance floor.

Opposite Traditional diamond-patterned stable paving bricks, within a path of old bricks, are richly textured and will last indefinitely.
Designer Mark Rumary

Bricks can be set flat, with more of the surface visible, or on edge. Different patterns or "bonds" affect the look and can be used to lead the eye in a particular direction. Herringbone tends to draw the eye in the direction of the bond. Basketweave has little directional emphasis and is therefore ideal in a static situation either within or forming the whole of a terrace or sitting area. Running bond is the easiest to lay and, depending on whether the pattern runs across or along, can slow or accelerate the view. In more solid courses, the bricks are laid side by side with the joints coinciding. It is a crisp, straightforward pattern that often looks excellent in a contemporary situation.

Stable paving bricks

As the name implies, these were originally used for stable floors and can sometimes still be found secondhand. Often intricately patterned, they were laid as part of a larger decorative design. Nowadays they are usually made in an embossed diamond pattern, resembling a bar of chocolate. They are normally dark blue or red, but occasionally you may find a cream that looks particularly good used in conjunction with slate. Fired to a very high temperature, stable paving bricks are frost-proof and highly durable. They provide excellent grip and can be used to great advantage on sloping paths and drives.

Right A deck is ideal for terracing over slopes or for roof gardens, where weight is a consideration. It can be used on virtually any site, as long as there is adequate ventilation beneath the structure – particularly important in temperate climates. It is easily cut to accommodate existing features, such as trees.
Design Leisuredeck Ltd

Below Railroad ties laid with slightly tapering joints form an attractive curved path. They are tough and versatile and can be used for many projects around the garden. In open areas, they are unlikely to become slippery with algae.
Designer Butch Joubert

Wood

Wood is a versatile floor material that looks sympathetic in gardens where fences and trellises are used for the walls of the outdoor room. Both soft and hard wood (from environmentally renewable sources) need to be sanded and treated with two or three coats of preservative. Wood stains are available, not only in browns and black but also in silver-grays, reds, and greens, all of which can look appropriate in the right situation.

Decks

This versatile and relatively cost-effective flooring has not found favor in temperate climates, because of the fear that it will rot. However, as long as there is adequate ventilation beneath the surface, it can last up to twenty-five years.

Keep the wood clear of the ground by laying the deck on a series of supporting joists bolted to upright posts. Use pressure-treated lumber and, if you use a tropical hardwood such as teak, ensure that it comes from a known and environmentally renewable source. The perfect link between a wood-clad house and the outside, a deck is also ideal for a roof garden, where weight must be minimized. If you have a garden that slopes steeply away from the house, consider a series of wooden decks, linked by wooden steps.

The flexibility of the material means that it can be built around existing trees, or rock outcrops or other awkwardly shaped features, such as pools. Boards can be laid in varying widths and at different angles to set up interesting visual rhythms or to echo those of adjoining structures. If a deck becomes slippery (rarely a problem in full sun), scrub the surface down with a weak solution of household bleach, making sure that it does not splash onto nearby plants.

Wood blocks

Originally used for street paving, these are available from specialist manufacturers and measure approximately 6x6x6in/150x150x150mm. Set them on a bed of sand and retain the edges with blocks set in concrete. Position them as close together as possible to provide a remarkably flat surface with wonderful textural detail. Longer blocks are available for steps and to edge raised beds. Complete the look with built-in or freestanding solidly built wooden garden furniture.

Wood chips

Produced when tree trunks or branches are ground down, wood chips are available in different grades, the largest pieces about 2in/50mm square, the smallest little more than fiber. (The latter can be used for soil conditioning, and makes an excellent substitute for peat.)

While the large chips can be unsightly, medium chips (about 1in/25mm in diameter) are ideal for paths in an informal part of a garden, or in a woodland area, and as a weed-suppressing mulch between and beneath plants. Spread them to a depth of about 2-3in/50-75mm and top them up as necessary. They also form an excellent play surface, eliminating worn lawns as well as bruised knees.

Synthetic materials

Some garden designers are now experimenting with synthetic flooring materials. They are easy to transport as well as being light and durable – particularly important for roof or balcony gardens. A wide range of plastics, of the kind used for sports areas and running tracks, is available. They come in a variety of colors and are as easy to lay as plastic flooring inside a house. Simply unroll them over a concrete screed or suspended floor. They can be laid smoothly across flat areas or up and down concrete ramps, eliminating steps. Being slightly resilient, they make an ideal surface for children or for elderly people.

Leading-edge garden design, like leading-edge architecture, is fun, and for a designer using synthetic flooring is like being released from a straitjacket. Different colors can swoop and turn in endless fascinating combinations. These plastics could be used in conjunction with materials such as polished fiberglass, polyester woven fences, and acrylics to produce compositions of great beauty. In these gardens of the future, holograms, lasers, and fiber optics will introduce a totally new dimension at night.

Above A wood chip path winding through a "woodland" area provides the perfect natural link with the surrounding planting and wooden fence in Frank Cabot's garden (see also pp.73, 126, 133).

Above A tranquil, smooth expanse of carefully tended lawn is surrounded by exuberant planting in many shades of green. This is a stunning juxtaposition of the tamed with the apparently unruly. Grass, because of its uniform color and texture, is a great unifier, even in the smallest garden, and where large areas are involved, as here, a grassy surface will tie many different elements together. *Designer Bruce Kelly*

Living materials

Lawns of grass and other ground-cover plants look and feel softer than paving, and some provide color and interest for much of the year. They are certainly the most cost-effective way of covering a large space, but they take time to establish and require ongoing maintenance. In design terms, an expanse of green carpet acts as a foil, playing a passive role in the garden's structure, and its shape and proportion need as much thought as any floorcovering.

Grass

Lawns are made up from a number of grass species and vary in quality from those that use very fine-leafed varieties, for a bowling-green effect, to those that include broader-leafed and tougher species that are better suited to a hard-wearing "utility" surface. Whether you choose sod or seed, always check the quality and grass mix to ensure the kind of lawn you want. Sods establish themselves far more quickly than seed, and are now available in such large sizes that it is almost as easy to lay a lawn as it is to roll out a carpet. They are, however, far more expensive than seed. Do not forget that grass is a plant like any other, and the ground it is to cover needs thorough cultivation before the grass is laid or sown. Regular fertilizing, weeding, watering, and scarifying are needed to maintain a healthy lawn. When mowing, do not make the mistake of cutting the grass too short; this only accelerates drying out and subsequent browning during dry weather. Use a reel lawn mower or one with a rear roller for the striped effect associated with an "English" lawn. This strong directional emphasis can be used as a design tool. A long, narrow lawn mown down its length seems even longer, so consider mowing across the space or at a diagonal to lead the eyes in another direction. Alternatively, in a larger garden with gentle contouring and planted areas, mowing can be carried out in a sweeping pattern that helps draw the eyes through and around the space.

In less formal parts of the garden and beneath trees, it can be attractive to allow grass to grow longer, and to introduce bulbs and wildflowers to provide color over many months. Establish a mowing regime that allows the bulbs to die down naturally and the wildflowers to set seed. If you buy wildflower and grass-seed mixtures, do not be surprised if, over a period of years, certain species die out and others predominate.

Ground covers

Many plants other than grass will knit together and form a good-looking carpet less than 6in/150mm high. Some of these, such as ivy, pachysandra, and epimedium, are extremely tough and tolerate shade that grass would find impossible, making them an attractive proposition for ground cover under trees. Once they are established, little work is required apart from occasional pruning, fertilizing, and clearing fallen leaves. Ivies can be planted in geometric patterns for a formal look in shady urban gardens.

Chamomile and thyme are other good alternatives to a lawn, but they do not wear very well. They will, however, tolerate the occasional knock from a football, which will serve to release their fragrance, and they can be planted to fill the joints in widely spaced paving and steps.

Of course, ground covers and vegetative floors need not necessarily all be planned to be walked on, and there are a large number of carpets that are a half way house between, for example, grass and a full-blown shrubbery. In a woodland, this kind of carpet might be bluebells, aconites, ivy, or honeysuckle, all of which could be walked through rather than on. A more controlled situation might involve sweeps of relatively delicate grasses and wildflowers such as poppies, cranesbill, vetch, and cornflowers.

Low-growing shrubs can form superb carpets: drifts of *Cistus* x *dansereaui* "Decumbens," helianthemum, *Cytisus* x *kewensis,* or *Hebe rakaiensis.* Spreading junipers, *Ceanothus thyrsiflorus repens*, ground-covering cotoneasters, and so on can either be used as groups or "lawns" of a single species or worked together as combination plantings.

Below Living floors need not be of grass. Here drifts of low-growing perennials including liriope and sedum merge to form a colorful carpet – though not one for walking on. The advantage of such planting is the variation of flower and foliage throughout the year, and even in winter it will look attractive. *Landscape Architects: Wolfgang Oehme and James Anthony van Sweden*

Water

Areas of water that take up a significant amount of space – at least 6x6ft/1.8x1.8m – can be considered as part of the floor of the outdoor room and part of the soft landscape. They can range from streams that run naturally through the garden to still expanses of water that rely for their effect on the reflections of the sky and surrounding planting or structures.

In many gardens, the lie of the land suggests the right location – a dip in the ground, a damp area, or a shallow valley that has the potential to be blocked at one end and filled with water. In a larger landscape, a stream could be dammed or an area excavated, and the spoil used to create gently contoured banks around the perimeter. This principle of cut and fill can also be used in far smaller gardens, providing you keep the changes in level gentle.

Water close to the house will almost certainly look better in a formal arrangement, while the farther from the building, the more informal it can become. My own garden (see plan on p.141) is set on a slope and uses water as an

Below Water is as important an element of the floor covering in this garden as the lawn, paving, and decks. In a large garden, as a general rule, the less formal the pool, the greater the distance from the house. On this sloping site, the sight and sound of water close to a sitting area gives great pleasure, and an informal pool, its lines concealed beneath a pebble beach, sits conveniently between the terrace and well-kept lawn.

important element. The long upper pool, set across the garden, together with the intermediate cascade and formally framed stream, help to make the composition feel much wider. Although the whole feature is entirely artificial, I have used the slope to best advantage and the composition looks comfortable.

The area is also generous, and one of the basic rules of water gardening is that the larger the pool, the easier it is to create a natural balance and a healthy environment for pond life. Water also, of course, offers the opportunity to grow a wide range of beautiful water-side and aquatic plants.

Nowadays the installation and maintenance of water features is relatively straightforward. Pools of various shapes can be bought molded in fiberglass, and flexible liners range from laminated plastics to butyl rubber, which may be guaranteed for more than twenty years. Whatever you use, make sure that the liner is completely hidden from sight behind or beneath the pond edge, whether of brickwork, stone, or soil. For larger pools, employ a landscape contractor experienced in construction and large-scale earth moving.

Below Still water offers the bonus of reflections and brings a feeling of calm to a composition. The planting is simple, a combination of green and white that forms a restful, undemanding background.

In the formal setting of this walled garden, the geometry of a square raised pool works well. Its edging of sturdy stone slabs is in harmony with the stone used on nearby walls. *Designer Michael Balston*

Above Steps can be a design feature in themselves, as well as serving a practical function. Concrete treads appear to float, giving this asymmetrical composition a feeling of lightness. The solidity of the slabs is offset by the delicacy of the ferns.

CHANGES IN LEVEL

Changes in level add interest to a garden and offer opportunities for imaginative as well as purely practical treatments. A bold sweep of broad steps, or steep terracing, edged with pots or punctuated by other garden ornaments can make a strong design statement. But the design possibilities do not stop there. A flight of steps need not necessarily be set square with the house or surrounding terrace; a diagonal flight up a slope can form a gentler gradient, while a landing can provide a pause, a place for ornaments, or a change of direction. On a flat site, you may want to contour the land to create gentle mounds and slopes, raised beds, or unobtrusive steps to add an element of dynamism.

Steps

All steps should be as broad and generous as possible, not only so that they become a feature in their own right, but also for safety's sake. People should be able to walk up and down comfortably, without breaking their stride. This means having a riser of approximately 6in/150mm and a tread of 18in/450mm. The treads should have a slight "fall," so that they shed water easily and if they overhang the riser by approximately 2in/50mm, they create a shadow line that helps soften the line of the flight. Safety is the main consideration, so if you are in any doubt about the construction, enroll the services of an expert.

The materials used should respect those used nearby, and, while a crisp, hard surface may be suitable close to the house, logs, railroad ties, or other lumber might suit a more informal area. Sometimes it is useful to give a visual warning of a change in level by laying a different material at the top of a flight. Thus a band of brick might form the edge of a top step, contrasting with adjoining precast paving or brushed concrete.

Right Sawn log sections, unobtrusively covered with chicken wire to prevent slipping, are firmly bedded into the ground and held in position with stakes – a picturesque and practical solution in an informal or woodland setting.

Slopes and ramps

The question of whether to grade sloping areas together by means of ramps rather than to terrace, using a retaining wall, must be considered at the design stage. In general, a wall should be used in a formal situation or where there is a particularly steep incline that needs terracing. If the slope is not too great, the garden will seem far more restful if the levels are graded together as much as possible, with planting softening any steeper, unmowable sections. In a small garden, retaining walls may look less comfortable, since they tend to subdivide the space and give an overworked impression.

Ramps need a greater length than steps to achieve the same height, and this must be taken into account at the planning stage; remember that a diagonal route is easier on a sharp incline. Ramps are usually informal, sometimes purely functional; but they may also be more architectural in concept, perhaps zigzagging down a slope in a geometric pattern that reflects the design of an adjoining terrace or other hard landscape feature. If a grass ramp is to link two lawned areas, make sure it is sufficiently wide to allow the passage of lawn mowers and wheelbarrows. A wide ramp not only looks better, it wears better too.

On very steep banks, there is always the possibility of soil erosion. Ground-cover planting helps minimize this. In extreme cases, a strip of webbing below the surface can help fix the soil. A further possibility is to use "crib-walling." This consists of a wooden or concrete lattice set into the bank at an angle. The lattice holds the slope in place while leaving room in the latticework for planting.

Elderly or disabled people as well as toddlers find hard-surfaced ramps easier to manage, but beware of smooth, precast slabs, which can become slippery when wet or in freezing weather. Choose instead a textured surface like brick, Belgian blocks, exposed aggregate, or tamped concrete.

Below Natural outcrops of stone anchor this informal flight of steps, both physically and visually, providing pivots on which it is hinged. It meanders up the slope to a lawn at the top, the carved wood retaining wall at a turning point providing a nicely theatrical touch in this Los Angeles garden.
Designer Rick Mosbaugh

Left An unusual and imaginative combination of steps and ramps breaks up a long expanse of lawn. The change of level is slight, but the line of bricks that marks each rise becomes a strong visual element in the overall design of this garden in South Africa (see also pp.15 and 30).

FINAL DESIGNS: FORM AND FUNCTION

Confident of making the appropriate choice of materials for the framework of your outdoor rooms, you are now in a position to work up your rough layouts (see p.43) into a final design. My roughs evolved into the three treatments shown here, in which the materials for walls, floors, and ceilings reflect the style and functions of each outdoor room. In the strongly Modernist asymmetrical design (left), floor shapes overlap to form a collage of different surfaces – paving, brick, gravel, water, and grass. The planting plan for this garden is shown on p.120. In the formal garden (center), clearly defined areas of lawn, gravel, and brushed aggregate on one side are mirrored on the other. In the informal garden (right), the soft landscape sets the style, dominated by the fluid shapes of lawn and planted beds.

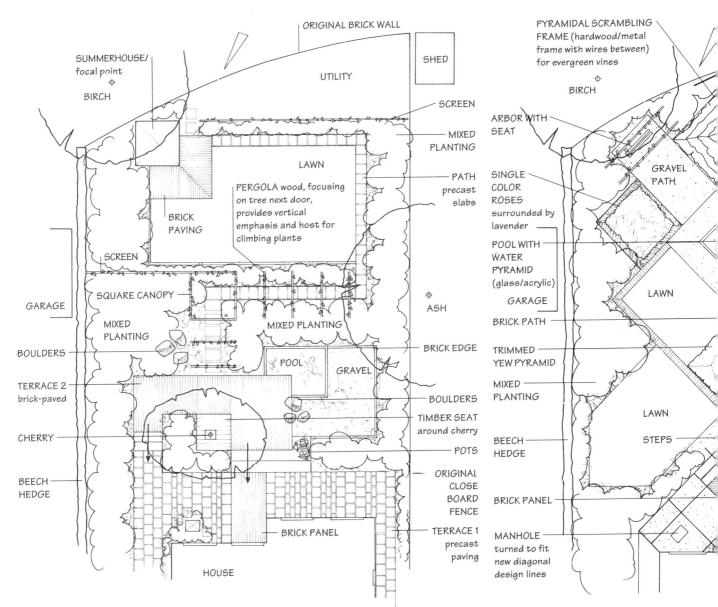

Structured informality (left)

Straight lines or rectangles convey purpose and create patterns. The terrace, in two sizes of precast paving brick, is laid in a staggered bond that leads the eyes out into the garden. A panel of paving bricks emphasizes the French windows and leads down the steps to a second brick–paved terrace. Planting divides the hard landscaped areas from the softer lawn, and the route of the path that links them maximizes the feeling of space.

Formal (center)

A modern approach to a formal design observes symmetry while turning the pattern at 45 degrees to the house. A panel of bricks emphasizes the steps down from the terrace, and a brick path leads between a pair of trimmed yew pyramids to the focus of the composition – a pool with a glass or acrylic water pyramid. Matching seats look back on this, and the pyramid shape is picked up again in the planting frame.

Informal (right)

Random rectangular paving, the least formal of all possible paving choices, is appropriately architectural next to the house. A deck surrounds the tree. Water will drain through it, so the roots below will not be affected. The design becomes more fluid as it moves away, and low mounds, partly built from the soil excavated for the pond, emphasize the flowing curve of the path that disappears from view, inviting exploration.

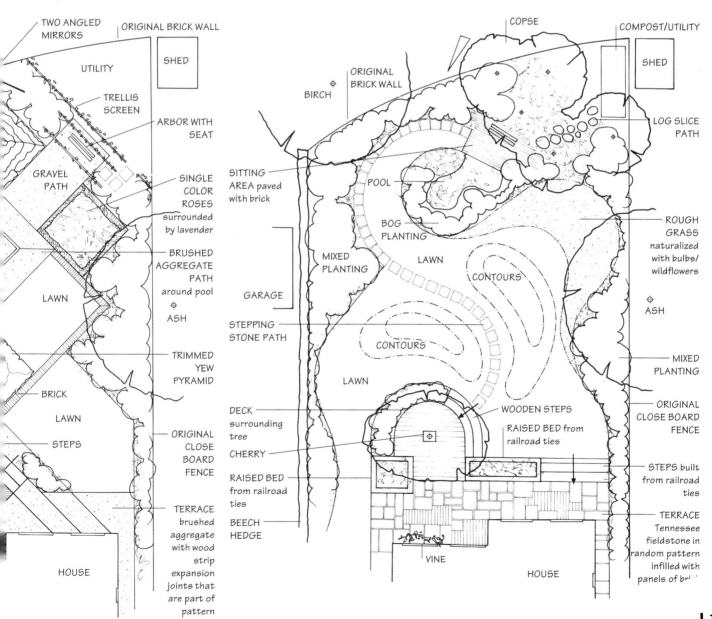

DECORATIONS AND FURNISHINGS

Decorating and furnishing rooms outdoors is every bit as pleasurable as it is indoors. And just as interior designers choose fabrics, furniture, pictures, and lighting to complement the treatment of walls and floors, so designers outside team furniture – tables, chairs, play equipment, barbecues – with the framework of the room. Think of the plants that add color, texture, and form as the soft furnishings of your outdoor room. Ornaments may range from decorative structures, such as summerhouses and gazebos, to fountains, statuary, or a simple cluster of terra-cotta pots. Imaginative lighting will enhance all these features as well as allowing you to enjoy your garden after dusk.

Previous pages Opulent and fragrant, *Wisteria floribunda* "Alba" cascading from a gray-blue pergola is the decorative focus of this simple terrace in a New Zealand garden.

The decorations and furnishings bring the outdoor room to life. Choose them to respect the overall theme and reflect your personality. *Designers John Tripp and Peter Masson*

The decorations and furnishings for your garden should emphasize the links, both physical and visual, with the house. Personal taste plays a part here: if your preference in the interior is for plain walls and the uncluttered look, carry that style out into the garden; if you like patterned wallpaper and bright chintzes, you will probably want a garden with plenty of color and ornament. To create this transition in a practical way is not easy, partly because we have been conditioned to think of the house and garden as separate spaces, and partly because fabrics and furniture suitable for outdoor use are not sold in settings that emphasize the links – alongside complementary interior furnishings. However, it is important to try to visualize the links and to make one's purchases with these in mind.

DECORATING PRINCIPLES

Many of the principles of interior decoration apply to the decorating of gardens. Generally, the understated and the simple are more interesting than the flamboyant and busy. Form is as important as color, because if outlines are ill-defined, color loses its impact. Rooms in which color and pattern predominate are hard to live with. Just as the heavily patterned wallpapers and fabrics that look more exciting than the plain ones in the shop sample book are often disappointing or frankly overpowering in your living room, so it is outdoors. Choose decorations and furnishings to complement the framework of your garden, for their suitability for your purposes and for the excellence of their construction. Touches of dramatic color are best if limited. When it comes to painting and decorating, think minimalist – most of the time.

Form and function

While the contours of garden furniture and features should sit comfortably within the framework, in decorating terms the most important forms are those of plants. How they relate to one another and to the garden structure are crucial elements in determining the rhythm and movement essential for a successful design. All have their own particular outline – prostrate, rounded, conical, weeping, spiky, and so on. A group of two or three plants of the same form will take on the overall shape of the individual species within it. Trees, for example, have specific outlines and, because of their size, their forms can dominate. Plan them to serve a function, too. A carefully sited conifer will make a punctuation point along a border. In the larger garden or landscape, Lombardy poplars, like fastigiate conifers, can be used in the same way as "key" plants. The architectural shape of a Scotch pine associates particularly well with the crisp line of any building and surrounding hard landscape details. Consider counterpoint, too – a weeping willow alongside a pond is a perfect example, with the vertically drooping branches set against the horizontal plane of water.

Classic plant combinations can be used to create rhythm and movement. The dome shape of *Hebe rakaiensis* set against a spiky yucca or cordyline with low ground cover such as *Cistus* x *dansereaui* "Decumbens;" in a larger space, the rounded flower heads of *Euphorbia characias wulfenii* combined with the sword-shaped leaves of phormium and the prostrate *Cotoneaster dammeri*. Shapes become increasingly important as the color scheme is simplified, so that if all color other than green is removed, the detailed form of leaves becomes more noticeable. Fennel planted with hosta and sedum will be dominated by their flower colors in late summer, but earlier in the year the contrast of the feathery foliage of the fennel with the rounded shiny leaves of the hosta and the fleshy leaves of the sedum will be the attention catcher.

Opposite Bold-leaved foliage plants form a decorative mantle, and their shapes are reflected in the pool. Simplicity is the keynote in floor and furnishing, and the color scheme is restrained. The contrasting textures of pebbles, wood, grass, and water make a subtle, but important, contribution to this balanced scheme.

Above Perimeter planting of the outdoor room usually combines a background of tough trees and shrubs with lighter, more decorative planting as infill.

The color, shape, and texture of leaves can be far more significant than flower color, and such classic combinations as purple and yellow – here purple cotinus with *Lonicera nitida* "Baggesen's Gold" – are always sucessful.

Right Drifts of color merge and overlap to create rhythm and continuity in a border at Bradenham Hall in Norfolk, England. Bold swaths are far more restful than numerous single plants, which invariably create an unsettled pattern.

Below Pale-pink Oriental poppies and rich blue delphiniums make a perfect combination against the neutral gray-green backdrop of *Pyrus salicifolia*.
Designer Christopher Grey-Wilson

Color

Obviously, using color opens up exciting possibilities for the garden decorator, not only in the choice of color schemes for fabrics and furniture but also, especially, when painting with plants. The basic rules apply: vibrant reds, oranges, and yellows draw the eye, while cooler hues such as soft blues, pinks, and purples increase the sense of space. Furniture painted in bright primary colors is best sited to make a deliberate statement: a vibrant red seat will be eye-catching set against the dark-green foliage of a hedge. In muted green it will blend with its surroundings. Indeed, green is also an excellent color for fabrics and sets up a particularly elegant dialogue with cream awnings or umbrellas. Strongly patterned and brightly colored seat covers may be ideal near the house, especially if they carry through a scheme from indoors, but if you use the same fabrics in a distant sitting area your eye will jump immediately to them with a subsequent foreshortening of the space. Similarly in planting, Gertrude Jekyll expounded the idea of keeping the hotter flower colors closer to the house and the cooler colors farther away. Sometimes, though, it is refreshing to make an occasional color break in a border, introducing, say, a vibrant dash of yellow in one that is predominantly pink and blue.

While gray- and silver-leaved plants are great harmonizers, whites and creams can be used as a specific counterpoint or highlight in a planting plan. But use brilliant white carefully for fabrics or on walls and furniture: in strong sunlight, it causes glare and casts crisp shadows. Off-white is a better choice: it mellows gracefully and the shadows it casts are cool rather than cold.

Do not forget the subtle effects that different shades of green can produce, or the striking contrasts of variegated leaves, the vibrancy of autumn color, the browns and silvers of ornamental grasses, and the color of winter stems and bark.

Visit established gardens and observe how colors are used. You will soon understand what makes some colors feel comfortable together, while other combinations produce an unsettling effect. Take photographs and notes and you will gradually get the confidence to create successful color schemes of your own.

PLANTING

If you think of the framework of your garden as the constant – the unpainted canvas of a picture – you are ready to build up the rest of the composition from an ever-changing pattern of living vegetation in the same way as an artist builds up a picture by mixing paints and applying them sparingly here, more thickly there.

Choose plants to provide interest throughout the year, but also make sure that the amount of maintenance they require is not burdensome, otherwise you will become a slave to your outdoor room. There are many ways to find the plants that will work best for you. You can prepare a planting plan simply from nurserymen's catalogs and a good plant directory that gives information on flower and foliage color, fragrance, time and duration of flowering period, and the plants' preferred soil and aspect. Supplement this with lists of plants that suit your specific situation, such as plants for seaside locations, for acidic soils, for full sun or deep shade, or for damp or dry conditions.

Planning a garden in this way is, however, not nearly as much fun as getting to know plants at first hand, just as shopping by catalog, though often convenient, is never as satisfactory as going into a store and being able to handle the goods. When it comes to fragrance, it is essential to "smell for yourself."

Garden centers and nurseries are an obvious place to start learning about plants at first hand, but plants are invariably small and do not give an idea of how they will develop. Display gardens at shows can be inspiring, but the danger here is that they are planted for immediate effect and with little regard to the plants' eventual size and how they will relate to one another after a period of time.

By far the best way to learn about plants is to see, touch (and smell) them growing, especially in botanical gardens where the species are clearly identified. Take a camera and notebook with you to record how large particular species grow and to build up a portfolio of what you like and of combinations of plants that you find pleasing. When you return to your initial garden survey, you will be able to apply the knowledge you have gained to your own particular garden conditions, and choose your new plants with confidence.

The planting plan

While the master plan of your garden shows the layout and framework, you will need a separate plan for the decorative planting. Enlarge your plan to scale so you have enough space to note plant names and quantities, then follow the sequence described below, which applies to virtually any garden, whatever its soil type or aspect. First, if you are redesigning an established garden, you will have noted any existing planting on the initial survey: decide which plants to remove and which to retain. In some cases, existing planting may provide you with a cue to follow for your new plan. Then "paint" a backbone of hardy and largely evergreen material – normally trees and shrubs that retain their shape throughout the year. Next, plan for an infill of smaller, more decorative shrubs and ground covers mixed with herbaceous or hardy perennial plants and bulbs. Finally, add the annuals and tender perennials, just as you might add some bright cushions to a room to give it a lift. Apart from specimen plants, it is often more satisfactory to work with groups of odd rather than even numbers of plants, so that the composition knits together as a balanced whole. This is a good general rule to follow when planting out or grouping containers.

The backbone

Use the backbone planting to transform the shape of your plot or to lead the eye in a particular direction. In a small garden, you may need only a few plants to reinforce the curve of a border or to take the eye past the sharp angle formed by two boundaries. Do not plant a single specimen in a sharp angle, because it will simply draw the eye and emphasize the awkwardness of the area rather than disguise it.

You can also place backbone plants at strategic points such as at the end of a long border, or to frame a feature such as a bench. Here, they perform the role of "key" plants, their architectural outlines providing a certain drama and acting as anchors to the design from which infill planting can spring. They also serve the purpose of disguising the boundaries and possibly forming a link with the trees and shrubs in adjoining gardens, thus making your plot appear larger. Not only the form of backbone plants but also the size and shape of their leaves will have an impact on how you perceive the space. Broad leaves, such as those of *Fatsia japonica* or *Vitis coignetiae,* are visually dominant, focusing the eye and tending to draw a boundary closer. The small, delicate leaves of *Fargesia nitida* or escallonia on the other hand help to maximize space by splitting the image into far more pieces and thus detracting from the background. As well as year-round foliage, they may have the bonus of attractive flowers and winter berries. Choose species that are relatively fast-growing, or interplant slower-growing evergreens with fast-growing deciduous species such as broom, buddleia, or lavatera: these are relatively short-lived and can be removed as the evergreens start to reach maturity.

Opposite Lush perimeter planting, mostly of tall shrubs, encompasses a small London garden, blurring the boundaries and ensuring privacy; lower, infill planting defines and divides the two garden rooms.

The progression of space is subtly handled, leading from the formality of a paved terrace next to the house through a brick-edged, closely mown lawn, around a central bed of mostly fragrant plants, to an area of rougher grass, naturalized with wildflowers at the end of the garden. The planting reinforces this pattern. The hard landscape is beautifully executed – and bricks form a practical mowing edge to the lawn.

Designer Arabella Lennox-Boyd

Above A rich mix of shrubs for year-round interest and hardy perennials for seasonal color show the importance of using both backbone and infill plants.

The provision of a wide path makes good sense if plants are to be allowed to spill over.

Opposite above John Brookes's bold use of architectural plants is combined with an eye for color in this corner of his own garden at Denmans in Sussex, England. Bridging the path with two clumps of purple sage adds continuity to the scheme. Staggered paving allows the two contrasting floor surfaces to run together.

The infill

Just as when you paint a wall in a plain background color and then sponge or stipple over it in a contrasting or complementary color you set up a dialogue between the two, so backbone planting needs an infill to set up a dialogue.

Infill plants also provide changing interest throughout the year. Here all your research, imagination, and sense of fun can come into play as you choose plants in favorite color schemes and in contrasting and complementary leaf shapes and textures. Remember, too, that the form, structure, and color of a particular species must also relate to its neighbors.

A mixed planting of shrubs with hardy perennials will supply far greater interest across the seasons than either group used alone, and is much less labor-intensive than a purely herbaceous infill planting. While herbaceous plants are helpful in supplying accent and color, shrubs provide a sense of maturity and help to support the taller-growing and laxer varieties of herbaceous plants.

Grasses are becoming increasingly popular and are another good choice as infill plants, providing you check that your soil type and climate are suitable. They provide year-round interest – many of them look spectacular in winter – as well as rhythmical movement and a delightfully restful noise when the wind blows through their foliage and stems.

Ground-cover plants knit together to form a carpet and suppress weed growth, but should not be thought of simply as a means of reducing garden maintenance. They play an important part in visually tying together an entire planting plan.

The range of bulbs that is available is enormous, so you can have these plants in flower in the garden right through the year. Forget the traditional serried ranks of

Below Ornamental grasses can provide shape and texture throughout the year, if seedheads are retained until growth restarts in spring. There are grasses for every situation, from arid to wet, some water-side species thriving on the edge of lakes, or, as here, on the banks of a stream.

tulips that are so much a part of municipal garden schemes. These work well in formal garden layouts, but for the most part go for high drama and plant large drifts of a single species. Some bulbs are labor-intensive, needing to be planted out in autumn and lifted when their leaves have died down. Many such as daffodils, narcissi, crocus, muscari, and alliums suit being "naturalized" – left in the ground to flower year after year. Either plant them together with other plants and shrubs in a border, or with wildflowers and other indigenous planting in rough, grassed areas out in the open or beneath trees.

Annuals and tender perennials planted out after the last frosts and cleared away before the winter cold serve the same purpose as bulbs, filling in the gaps as plantings mature and adding splashes of instant color. Plant them in bold blocks of color for dramatic effects in pots and containers that can be moved around.

Far left The shape of flower heads – here spherical alliums and upright polygonums – is often as important as the color.
Designer Christopher Grey-Wilson

Left Annuals are useful for filling gaps with instant summer color. Petunias, impatiens, and verbena make a colorful carpet planted in front of the statice and cosmos.

119

Planting plays an important role in softening the geometry of this asymmetric design (see p. 108), as well as providing continuity as you move through the space. Because the house and terrace are on a slightly higher level than the garden, the pattern of the planting is thrown into sharp relief, making it all the more important to place hot and cool colors with care.

Only a few different species are used, but there are a relatively high number of plants in each group of backbone plants as well as in the drifts of smaller infill plants. Their planting positions reinforce the underlying hard landscape structure and the difference between backbone and infill material is clear.

The screen and pergola provide vertical emphasis, break the sightline sufficiently to draw attention away from the neighbor's shed, and, when disguised with foliage, divide the top and bottom of the garden. From the terrace, the neighboring garage will be hidden from view by the tall-growing *Elaeagnus* x *ebbingei*.

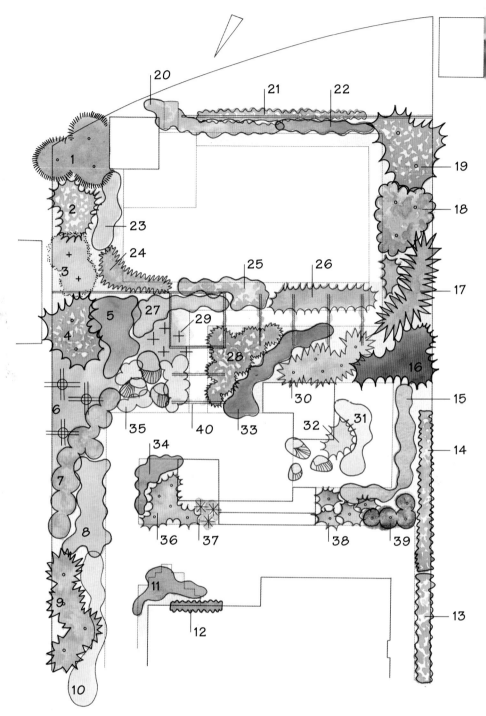

1 3 *Corylus maxima* "Purpurea" (B)	11 Annual color
2 3 *Aruncus dioicus*	12 1 *Lonicera sempervirens*
3 2 *Fargesia nitida* (B)	"Dropmore Scarlet"
4 2 *Choisya ternata* (B)	13 1 *Clematis montana wilsonii* (B)
5 10 *Anchusa azurea*	14 1 *Passiflora caerulea* (B)
"Loddon Royalist"	15 14 *Echinops ritro*
6 6 *Elaeagnus* x *ebbingei* (B)	16 2 *Cotinus coggygria*
7 8 *Senecio greyi*	"Royal Purple" (B)
8 11 *Rudbeckia deamii*	17 6 *Miscanthus sinensis* (B)
9 4 *Elaeagnus pungens* "Maculata" (B)	18 3 *Lavatera* "Rosea" (B)
10 18 *Anthemis tinctoria*	19 2 *Choisya ternata* (B)
"E.C. Buxton"	20 15 *Symphytum peregrinum*

21 2 *Lonicera japonica* "Halliana"	32 3 *Salix helvetica*
22 8 *Brunnera macrophylla*	33 25 *Salvia* x *superba*
23 9 *Digitalis grandiflora (ambigua)*	34 9 *Geum* "Mrs. G. Bradshaw"
24 11 *Dicentra formosa*	35 8 *Genista lydia*
"Stuart Boothman"	36 5 *Skimmia japonica* "Rubella"
25 12 *Iris sibirica* "Papillon"	37 3 *Dicentra purpurea* var. *albiflora*
26 24 *Eryngium alpinum*	38 4 *Perovskia atriplicifolia*
27 12 *Heuchera* "Rosemary Bloom"	39 4 *Verbascum* "Gainsborough"
28 11 *Hebe rakaiensis*	40 Pergola and screen covered
29 6 *Hosta sieboldiana* var. *elegans*	with a combination of white
30 5 *Hypericum* "Hidcote"	wisteria and laburnum
31 8 *Kniphofia* "Maid of Orleans"	(B) denotes "Backbone" plants

Fragrance

The importance of fragrance in a garden is often overlooked or at best treated at random, but ideally you should incorporate "fragrance zones" in your plan at the outset. Most plants need warmth to reveal their scent and sheltered spots where strong winds will not disperse it. The obvious places for fragrance zones, then, are in sheltered places or near to the house or to sitting areas, so the perfume can be enjoyed as you relax or eat in the garden. On warm summer's evenings, with doors and windows thrown open, some of the scent will waft inside. Other useful places for plants with scented flowers or foliage is near entrances, along paths, or at a turning point where you will brush against the plant as you walk, releasing the fragrance as you do so.

Whatever the garden's situation, there is a scented plant that will suit. Some of the best are old favorites such as jasmine, stock, nicotiana, rosemary, lavender, and honeysuckle.

Below A clump of lavender is strategically sited at the top of the steps and at a curve in the path, where passersby will brush into it.

Here planting softens the hard landscape and change in level, acting as a pivot for the brick path that sweeps away beneath the pergola, planted with fragrant roses.

The background planting of trees and large shrubs provides screening and privacy, while the thatched gazebo is a delightful focal point.
Designer David Stevens

Left Nicotiana and sweet-smelling herbs fill a small front garden in London with fragrance, particularly in the evening.

Since many herbs are rampant, it is a good idea to plant them within a contained area, and this brick path is both decorative and practical. Dead-heading will prolong the display of nicotiana, and regular applications of a liquid fertilizer will maintain vigor.
Designer Michael Runge

FURNITURE AND FABRICS

Imagine a living room in your house without anywhere to sit down, a dining room with no table, or a rumpus room without any toys, and you will appreciate that garden furniture is an essential ingredient of your outdoor room. It will not only complete the decoration but also double the enjoyment you get out of your garden, enticing you outside on less-than-perfect days, providing extra space for entertaining, giving you somewhere ideal for relaxation, or encouraging the children to play in the open air.

Style and purpose

The range of outdoor furniture is almost as wide and varied as that for indoors, but generally speaking it is less comfortable, and often downright uncomfortable. Nevertheless, you should allow outlines and styles to govern your choice if a chair or bench is to play an ornamental role – to provide a focal point at the end of a vista, to add a rustic note in a woodland area, or to punctuate a long border with seats set in bays. Traditional wrought iron looks appropriate in a period setting and classic reproduction stone seats and benches will suit a formal design. Seats and tables made of sawn tree trunks will enhance an informal garden area, and wheelbarrow seats that can be trundled from place to place add a note of humor.

When it comes to sitting and relaxation, however, comfort is more important than style. Try out tables and chairs as you would when choosing your dining-

Above Pretty as well as practical, these bentwood chairs, framed by the stone urns flanking the end of the terrace, are the focal point of a casual composition.

Right Wooden furniture harmonizes with the wooden deck and steps in the garden of my old friend Steve Lorton in Seattle. The design is measured but not austere, with a strong sense of style and purpose. This is the perfect yard, relaxed, functional, and private.

room furniture: make sure knees fit under tables and the chairs are the right height. Furniture for relaxing is not worth having unless you can lounge in it. Try before you buy, and, if it is tough enough to withstand the elements and will also blend with your garden style, then you will be making the right choice.

Cushions increase the comfort of all garden seats, whether rustic wood or elegant cane and wicker, and in hot weather are virtually essential on metal and plastic furniture. Choose fabrics that extend links with indoors by carrying through the same or toning colors. The classic beige or green of canvas-covered seating – upright director's chairs and casual deckchairs – blend well in any garden setting, or you may prefer to make your own covers in a color that picks up on schemes used elsewhere.

Parasols and umbrellas provide welcome shade on hot sunny days and a certain amount of shelter in a light shower. Like ceilings, they bring a feeling of intimacy to entertaining, dining, and play areas. They must be anchored firmly against sudden gusts of wind but should be easy to whisk away in stormy weather. Beige or honey-colored fabrics tone down sunlight without being obtrusive, though patterns can work well if chosen specifically to make a design statement – bold stripes, for example, to echo a slatted fence.

Above White furniture, simple in style, echoes the white painted woodwork on the house. I designed this terrace so that it is slightly elevated, thus separating the sitting and dining area from the lawn and forming a self-contained outdoor room.

The space is intimately enclosed by planting, including a fragrant lavender, while vines soften the façad of the house.

Opposite A chic approach to color teams chairs and shutters in a pale blue-green that picks up the mottled hues of the plane-tree trunks. *Designer Jean Mus*

The choice of furniture for cooking or playing, which further exploits your garden as a place in which to live and entertain your friends, also depends more on function than style. Barbecues and play equipment must be designed and positioned to be safe, but aim for an affinity of style for the area in which they are sited or built. If brick is used for the construction, for example, it should match the bricks used for walls or paving. The type of barbecue will depend on how often you will use it, the size of your garden, and your budget. Avoid a sophisticated arrangement unless you plan to cook outside almost every day in summer. A simple portable barbecue will fit in anywhere and is easy to store away.

For children, a paved area near the house, if it is large enough, can be used for riding tricycles or playing skipping games. A built-in sandbox with a removable cover will be an asset. Climbing frames and swings, a play or tree house – all make permanent play furniture that, if well designed, will offer hours of fun.

Above left Simple furniture often looks better and is more comfortable than that of complicated design. Canvas is a sensible choice for outdoors, and gray blends well with any setting. Alongside navy, the result is stylish.

Above right A warm yellow awning provides a sunny note in this New York roof garden, even when skies are gray. As well as reducing glare, it offers shelter and privacy.

SPECIAL FEATURES

You can stamp your own personality on your garden design with the use of statues, murals, pots and containers, or unusual garden buildings. Some, like a water feature or a summerhouse, can stand as focal points in their own right, while others, like special lighting effects, serve to complement and enhance your garden's features while extending the amount of time you can get enjoyment in the area. Do not be tempted to pile on feature after feature in an attempt to add drama to the scene. The viewer will be overwhelmed and will not know where to look next. It is far better to plan for one or two clear, simple statements that, by their very simplicity, will add the drama you are looking for.

Below A delightful arbor transforms this corner of Stonecrop, Frank Cabot's garden, into a secluded sitting room. Well-detailed, with the line of the built-in seat echoing that of the main structure, its architectural quality is softened by planting.

Right Delicate, almost frivolous, this pretty little gazebo is bound to catch the eye. The sitting area is framed, but not screened, by the low hedge in a New Zealand garden.

Garden buildings

Whatever their purpose, garden buildings are among the largest and therefore the most dominant elements in the garden. Broadly speaking, they can be divided between the utilitarian and the decorative. Some, such as those adjoining a swimming pool, can be multifunctional, including facilities for changing and entertaining with a sauna and jacuzzi, as well as a filtration plant. Many prefabricated buildings are available, but choose with care as some of them are flimsily made and poorly designed. If you can afford it, it is often better to have one specially designed and made.

Plan for greenhouses, sheds, and storage units – the purely utilitarian buildings you are likely to need – to have an ample area around them as work and access space. Sheds may need to be close to a vegetable plot for the storage of tools. For general storage of household overspill, bikes, and baby carriages, they may need to be fairly large and are better near to the house: if so, they should be purpose-built in brick or wood to form a visual extension of the house they adjoin. Soften the outline if you wish with a trellis cladding, or with wires, to support vines.

Of all the decorative garden buildings, the gazebo is probably the least understood. It is a small building positioned specifically to embrace a view. The style of a gazebo can be anything from a half-timbered thatched construction to an ultramodern steel-and-glass structure, depending on the style of your house and garden. Whatever the style, remember that a gazebo will draw you toward it and that the view from it should be worth embracing.

Summerhouses provide shelter and a place to sit some way from the house, where the garden can be appreciated. Site one in a secluded corner with a sitting area, perhaps with a path leading to it. Similarly, frames for climbing plants in the form of arbors and bowers are usually set in a quiet part of the garden, where you can relax under a cover of foliage and flowers. Reached by a path, an arbor will often become a major focal point and, as a general rule, the more generous its size the more comfortably it will sit in its surroundings and the more easily it will accommodate a seat within it. Ready-made wood and metal arbors are available, but it is relatively simple to construct one from lumber uprights and overheads faced with trellis panels or wires to support vines. Stone or brick pillars make an elegant framework, but are more difficult to create.

Generally speaking, a folly is an amusing but useless copy of some other building – part of a ruined castle for instance, an inland lighthouse, or a massive pigpen in the Doric style – that is intended as a focal point in a garden. As they really need to be viewed from a distance, a garden or estate of some considerable size is necessary. A treehouse for adults might be the equivalent of a modern folly. Although usually designed for children, if you have a large enough tree or group of trees, building one as a summer dining room would be eccentric, and fun.

Below High drama is usually best achieved with utter simplicity. The white seat nestling under an arbor clothed in white roses is both a focal point and an irresistible resting place, at the end of a long hedged walk. *Designer Christopher Masson*

Above An arbor is a vehicle for the plants trained over it; it should be sturdy enough to bear their weight, and undemonstrative in design so that it does not compete for attention. Here two pots of fine hostas complete the feeling of leafy seclusion.

Above Three heads are clearly better than one in this situation, contributing a refreshing note to the top terrace of a Mediterranean garden (see p.92). Bold lilies and ligularias complement the feature's architectural precision. *Designer Claus Scheinert*

Opposite A millstone mounted on a sturdy pier is the focus of this richly planted pool. Water is pumped up through the hole in the middle and flows back to be recirculated. *Designer Richard Bödeker*

Rignt What greater pleasure than to soak in a hot tub surrounded by beautiful plants? A feature such as this could be incorporated into the smallest of gardens. *Designer David Stevens*

Water features

The sound and movement of water can bring a whole new dimension of enjoyment to a garden, and you do not need to have a large plot to benefit. As well as informal ponds and formal pools, there are many small water features that make fine focal points in today's gardens, some of which are described below.

A tank, a submersible pump, and a pipe for the water flow form the basis of many simple but attractive fountains. For example, a millstone fountain, with water pumped up through the hole in the stone, looks elegant in virtually any setting. Using similar mechanics, make a fountain from a terra-cotta or other pot placed on its side with water bubbling over the lip.

Where space is very limited, a small wall fountain may be an ideal feature. For a formal or period setting, masks and statues in a classical style are available in cast stone. For a sense of fun and excitement in a modern setting, choose from the more contemporary fountains that are available in materials ranging from concrete to acrylic.

Water staircases are the contemporary answer to a series of waterfalls. I have recently designed one in the form of an acrylic pyramid, which has water falling down its sides over a series of lips. The whole feature will be surrounded by a reflecting pool and, outside that, satellite pyramids of cascading plants will complete the picture.

Kugels are perhaps one of the most stunning water features ever produced. They consist of a polished sphere of granite up to two yards/meters across that floats on low-pressure jets of water pumped through a perfectly fitting granite cup. The ball floats and turns gently as valves operate to change the force of the supporting jets. They are perfectly safe, even for children, as the gap between ball and cup is too small for fingers to be trapped.

More practical water features can also take their place in the garden. Hot tubs or jacuzzis can easily be integrated into the overall design and become attractive features in their own right.

Rock features

If you want to incorporate a rock feature into your garden, remember the main rule is to make it look as if it has always been there. This means using local stone wherever possible and setting the stone so that it simulates a strata pattern as it outcrops above ground. Ideally, you should have a sloping site, which will be easier to deal with and will look more natural, but it is possible to work with a flat site, importing topsoil, and creating contours.

Choose a sunny slope and select the pieces of stone you want from a good stone merchant. It is better to use a limited number of large stones rather than a mass of smaller stones. Select a "key" stone and bed it into the slope at a slight angle or "bedding plane." This stone sets the angle for all the other rocks used. To make the simulation more authentic, site one or more "outlying" groups a short distance from the main feature to indicate further strata breaking through the surface at different points.

Setting rocks is an art, so if you use a contractor make sure you see examples of his work before starting. If you do the work yourself, make sure you are up to it, because the physical strain involved is considerable.

Right Stability, solidity, and continuity are important design elements in this composition. There is enormous power in the choice and siting of such massive rocks, which seem to compel you up the steps built in a combination of Belgian blocks and old railroad ties. Movement is generated by the diagonal line of the flight, and mystery is introduced as the view disappears around the corner.

Designer Richard Bödeker

Wall features

Wall features have a long and distinguished pedigree in the history of garden design. Some forms of ornament are built into the wall at the construction stage. The moongate, a device borrowed from the Far East, is a circular gap in a wall built to embrace a view of the wider landscape or another part of the garden. A small square gap in a wall can be covered with a grille to make a window feature. Other forms of ornament may be applied to the surface – shells, pebbles, ceramic dishes, wall planters, and plaques. Visual tricks using murals, mosaics, mirrors, and *trompe l'oeil* set out to create an illusion, which brings with it a feeling of space, mystery, surprise, and often humor – all important design elements inside or outside the house. Cleverly used, they are particularly effective in small gardens where there is a need to maximize space and where dramatic tension can be set up. You can achieve a simple *trompe l'oeil* effect by painting or fitting trellis to a wall to create a false sense of perspective. Add a painting of a slightly open false door or window to give the impression of access to an area beyond and, for even more trickery, paint the view through the window or doorway or use carefully placed mirrors to reflect the real planting surrounding the false doorway. Set mirrors at a slight angle from the main viewpoint, otherwise the onlooker will be visible in the mirror and the illusion will be lost.

The straightforward use of mirrors is a way of artificially creating a sense of space. Set a mirror behind a pool or other water feature, or run a wall of mirror glass or metalized polyester from inside to out to create an illusion and, at the same time, to link house and garden. If you have a sense of humor, try using fairground mirrors. This can be particularly amusing at the end of pathways, to distort the image of any oncomers and, understandably, this effect is particularly popular with children.

A well-painted mural can be startlingly realistic. Paint one to cover a whole wall, run beneath a verandah, and even continue into the house. The choice of scene is limited only by your imagination. You can have a harbor view, a broad country landscape, a view over a municipal garden, or simply a painting of plants and vines that can blend with the real thing growing in front. Murals can merge fact and fantasy: build a small wall in front of a larger one, then paint a cat sitting on top of the wall behind. When a real cat comes to join the painted cat on top of the wall, the illusion is complete! Windows can be painted on large blank walls to excellent effect, visually interrupting the area. Real window boxes can be fitted to add humor as well as an excuse to further enliven the wall with planting.

For a special feature that has, for centuries, been used indoors and out, choose a mosaic. Made from random-sized or regular pieces of glass or tile, they can be woven into formal or informal patterns or into scenes and pictures. Use them on walls or floor for a virtually indestructible, weather-resistant finish.

Below A moongate is a useful device for framing and visually linking two areas. In the Japanese garden at Lambeth Palace, England, foliage softens the line, drawing the eye past rough-hewn boulders to the glazed urn and smooth cobbles in the next room.
Designers Geoff and Faith Whiten

Left A misty morning in late summer at Stonecrop (see pp.73, 101, 126) transports the garden into a different world. Wooden obelisks act as hosts to climbing plants within the richly planted mixed borders.

Below The primitive solidity of this simple sculpture sits well in the wild garden at Shute House in Dorset, England.

Ornaments

These need to be positively sited in your garden plan and often the position is immediately obvious – a statue at the turn of a path, a freestanding sundial or armillary sphere at the cross-axis of two paths, or a pair of pots flanking a transition point. Occasionally though, the position is not immediately obvious and only as time passes will you realize the need for an ornament in a specific spot.

Statuary

Just what ornament you choose will, in part, be driven by the overall style of your garden and in part by your taste. Classical urns and statuary sit comfortably in a formal layout, framing a doorway or flight of steps, while contemporary ornaments feel naturally more at home in a modern or asymmetric setting. If you are confident with your taste, though, there is nothing to say that you cannot successfully mix the two. Choose materials to link with other parts of the house or garden, for example placing stone urns alongside stone walls or using terra-cotta to blend with the color of paving bricks or walls. Humor can also be brought into play in your choice of ornaments. A sculpted cat, for example, chasing a butterfly or dipping its paw into a pool adds a sense of fun and movement, as do sculptures of children playing, while a garden gnome might be your way of cocking a snook at the garden snobs.

In all probability, you may want one or two pieces to be very special, not necessarily in terms of cost, but in their position in the overall layout. A column or obelisk at the end of a pergola, a statue at the center of a pool, a clean, modern sculpture in the middle of a sweeping lawn, or a simple stone bowl that looks just right in a cottage-style garden, all need to be chosen with care for the special effect that they will make.

Opposite The romantic style of the sundial is reflected in the backdrop of crambe, roses, and lamb's ears in the white garden at Hazleby House. This is a fine partnership of manmade ornament and planting.

Pots and containers

Every garden, whatever its size, shape, or style, can be enhanced by pots and containers. They are immensely adaptable, providing the only possibility for planting for apartment-dwellers or on balconies, roof gardens, and houseboats, broadening the scope for planting in small yard and urban gardens, or making possible the growing of plants that require special soil such as the less rampant acidic-loving rhododendrons, azaleas, and camellias. In fact, there is very little you cannot grow in containers, providing you water and fertilize regularly.

Pots are excellent for both bulbs and summer bedding. Use them to give instant color to a terrace or patio, or in a garden that is new while you are waiting for the more permanent plants to develop.

How you position them is important, too. They can frame a broad flight of

Below Stone whippets guard the containers framing the doorway in this South African garden. Standard orange trees in terra-cotta pots, underplanted with white violas, flank the path against a backdrop of hanging grapevines. The simple floor unites the composition.
Designer Keith Kirsten

steps, guide the eye away from a dull corner, or form the focal point at the end of a path before it turns in another direction. Or use them as in the Far East, often grouped in bold blocks or ranks of fifty or more to create an entire garden set higher than the surrounding area.

The range of possible containers is endless, including even old pails, coal scuttles, and bathtubs. The main point to consider is, as always, suitability for the surroundings. Fiberglass containers in primary colors will look absurd outside an Elizabethan or Georgian façade, while wooden half-barrels painted white with black bands are perfect in a cottage-style garden. Remember, too, that in many instances the container is just a vehicle for the plant material and, as such, is almost always subservient to it. As a general rule, the larger the container, the happier the plant.

Below left The largest pots often need the simplest planting, or no planting at all. The shape of this Cretan wine jar is echoed by the simple line of the metal frame that supports a climbing rose. This simple arrangement makes an intriguing focal point in a quiet corner of the garden.

Above A large container planted with annuals is surrounded by smaller terra-cotta pots planted with tall agapanthus to make a colorful focal point. Grouping similar pots in this way has great impact.
Designer Ann Alexander-Sinclair

Above Lights set in the branches of trees shine down and create "moonlighting." Here the tracery of branches appears to float above the ground, leaving the lower trunks in a pool of darkness. The same garden can be seen in natural light on p.33.

A subdued background source of light is all that is necessary to transform a garden into an evening living room, since the eyes quickly adjust to the level supplied.

Designer Andrew Pfeiffer

Lighting

Garden lighting is either functional – to light driveways, paths, parking areas, and doorways – or decorative – to add atmosphere and special effects to plants, water features, and hard landscaping. It needs to be installed by a licensed electrician, and for sophisticated decorative lighting, which is fast becoming an art form, you will need to seek the advice of a designer who may well have been trained in interior or theater lighting.

Functional lighting should be unostentatious and merge with its surroundings. Remember that it is the emitted light that is important, so fittings should be simple and well-designed. Safety lighting for entrances, driveways, and parking areas is usually fitted at a high level to illuminate the entire area. To light up terraces and seating areas, the source should be below eye level to avoid dazzle. For steps, there are fittings that can be recessed into the riser or into the retaining walls on either side. Paths are often best lit at low level: incorporate lighting into the planting that lines the route.

Decorative lighting creates an entirely new dimension, with plants and features illuminated from below and behind to create silhouettes or focal points highlighted with spotlighting. Uplighting beneath a tree will pick out its whole structure. If you have a well, try setting lights at the top shining down. These create drama, because the light is reflected back from the water below and makes a gentle pool of illumination that seems to hover above the well.

Subtlety is all-important. Do not try to illuminate the whole of your garden at

Left Low-level lighting, positioned
to illuminate the plants, pots, and
central water feature, endows this
architectural composition with an
ethereal magic.

The deck and natural stone slabs
are set on the diagonal, increasing the
apparent width of a long, narrow
garden. The paving is "grazed" to
highlight the raked-out joints and
emphasize the pattern.

once: instead aim to create pools of light that unfold as you move through the
space. For winter, choose a group of dramatic winter stems or a tree with a bold
outline and throw them into relief with a gentle glow of light.

One of the most subtle and beautiful techniques is moonlighting, where several
low-voltage lamps shed a diffused light down from the upper parts of trees, causing
them to cast their shadows on a smooth lawn or paved area.

To highlight the texture of stone or the architectural detail of a fine façade, use
a lighting technique known as grazing. Here, fittings placed close to the wall or
other structures cast their light vertically up or down its face. Clothe trees in tiny
white, low-wattage bulbs. This looks charming, since the trees sparkle and the
lights dance in the breeze.

White light is not the only possibility for decorative use in your garden. Blue
filters can give breathtaking results, but be careful of red, yellow, and green, since
these turn foliage an unnatural and unattractive color.

Futuristic lighting

Lighting techniques of the future include the use of lasers, fiber optics, plasma
spheres, and holograms. Lasers can create pencil-thin beams of light, or revolving
swathes of light set in cones and tubes. Fiber optics can be used to light water, since
they carry no power down their length, hence there is no risk of electric shock. To
give the dramatic effect of caged lightning, use plasma spheres – glass balls filled
with inert gases that glow in the dark. In the correct setting, special effects created
by modern technology can, and should, enhance a garden design.

WELL-DESIGNED GARDENS

Well-designed gardens are the result of much careful thought and planning. They do not just "happen." I am still working on my own garden, and I discuss the development of its design in the following pages. It comes very close to my ideal: it relates perfectly to its site, reflects my own design preferences, and meets all the needs of my family.

The other gardens featured here present a diversity of styles, exploiting to the full a range of sites, urban and rural, in different parts of the globe. Each is unique in its approach, each has something special to offer. Draw from them, as I have done, that other vital ingredient of all the best designs: inspiration.

My ideal garden: the design

Choosing my own house and garden was far from easy. I wanted an orientation that provided plenty of sunlight, a sheltered location, and the possibility of linking house and garden in an intimate relationship. Family, too, had to be not only taken into account but positively involved with the planning process. Pauline, my wife, is a nongardener but a great garden user, my philosophy entirely. My son, a budding marksman, needed his own shooting range, at a safe remove from the house, near the top of the garden, while our daughter, who is at college, brings home lots of exuberant friends, and loves barbecues and sunbathing. Clearly we needed several outdoor rooms with different functions. Eventually I found an amply sized but derelict stone house with barn, garage, and about half an acre of land.

The ground sloped relatively steeply from west to east with a fall of about 7ft/2m, and the position of the building in the northeast corner of the plot meant that the sun swung around the house throughout the day, ensuring that there would always be somewhere sunny to sit. The views were wonderful, the soil variable with good patches running in with heavy clay, and a pH just on the acidic side of neutral.

Although the site, lying in a shallow valley, is comparatively sheltered, additional shelter would be important both from the wind, which could sweep in across the fields from the southwest with some ferocity, and from a lane that runs around two sides of the property. The only real solution was to build a stone wall, but it would have to be over 7ft/2m high, running for about 328yd/100m, and hence very costly. After much deliberation it was built, and I am convinced it was the right decision.

After shelter, my main aim was to create a series of outdoor rooms, which would need eventually as little maintenance as possible. The slope was a bonus as I wanted water (and lots of it), which always suits a sloping site. The

bank stopped very close to the house and needed cutting back with heavy machinery to create enough space for sitting, dining, and access around the building. I also needed access to the garage at the top of the garden.

The first job was the basic subdivision of space. I made a strongly linear structure, terracing the slope to create a series of platforms; these would be given over to combinations of planting, lawns, water, and hard surfaces.

There is a logical sequence to building any garden that allows each stage to be built without disrupting the last, and this certainly applied to mine. The framework of hard landscape elements, such as paths for access and terraces for sitting, were implemented first, although they inevitably take the lion's share of the budget. It also makes sense to make the rest of the framework – for example, building internal walls and marking out borders and other areas – at the same time, or next, as this forms the basis into and around which lawns, plants, and incidental features such as pergolas, pools, arbors, and garden buildings can be fitted. I constructed my pool, raised beds, and pergola at this stage, and followed up with the sodding and planting. Of course, incidental features can be added as time and money permit, but their position and the provision of access should be worked out and allocated at the design stage, and the space they are to occupy filled with temporary planting.

Any garden needs positive theming, and in mine this is provided by a combination of the hard landscape structure and water that runs throughout a large part of the composition. Paving and walling are partly in brick and

Previous pages A Californian garden designed by Garrett Eckbo retains some original paving and overhead beams. Chris Rosmini redesigned the garden to meet changing needs (see pp.152-157).

Opposite The design of my own garden reflects my passion for geometry and the manipulation of space. The entire composition is built up from a series of rectangles that seem to slide over one another, and which are surfaced in different materials – stone, brick, gravel, water, grass, and so on. Indeed, water plays a centrally important role, exploiting the slope to the best advantage, while plants, used for their sculptural and textural qualities, temper the underlying geometry.

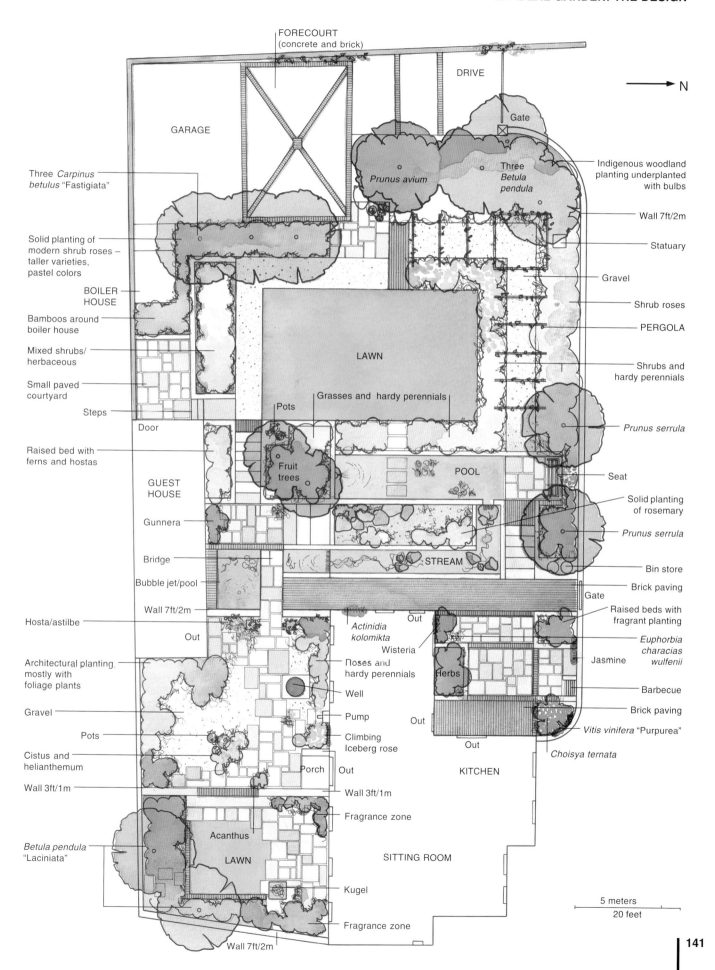

FORECOURT
(concrete and brick)

DRIVE

N

GARAGE

Gate

Prunus avium

Three
*Betula
pendula*

Indigenous woodland
planting underplanted
with bulbs

Three *Carpinus
betulus* "Fastigiata"

Wall 7ft/2m

Statuary

Solid planting of
modern shrub roses –
taller varieties,
pastel colors

Gravel

Shrub roses

BOILER
HOUSE

PERGOLA

Bamboos around
boiler house

LAWN

Shrubs and
hardy perennials

Mixed shrubs/
herbaceous

Small paved
courtyard

Grasses and hardy perennials

Prunus serrula

Steps

Pots

Door

Seat

Raised bed with
ferns and hostas

POOL

Fruit
trees

Solid planting
of rosemary

GUEST
HOUSE

Prunus serrula

Gunnera

Bridge

STREAM

Bin store

Bubble jet/pool

Brick paving

Wall 7ft/2m

Gate

Hosta/astilbe

Out

Raised beds with
fragrant planting

Out

*Actinidia
kolomikta*

*Euphorbia
characias
wulfenii*

Architectural planting,
mostly with
foliage plants

Wisteria

Roses and
hardy perennials

Herbs

Jasmine

Gravel

Well

Barbecue

Pots

Pump

Out

Brick paving

Cistus and
helianthemum

Climbing
Iceberg rose

Vitis vinifera "Purpurea"

Wall 3ft/1m

Porch

Out

KITCHEN

Choisya ternata

Wall 3ft/1m

Fragrance zone

Betula pendula
"Laciniata"

Acanthus

LAWN

SITTING ROOM

Kugel

5 meters

20 feet

Fragrance zone

Wall 7ft/2m

partly in stone; both materials are used for the house and also reinforce the strongly linear theme. The slabs are in fact reproduction stone, but of a quality that makes it difficult to tell apart from the real thing.

Connection and continuity between house and garden is of vital importance. The barn – now our guest house – which lay to the south both felt and looked isolated, so I built another high wall with a gateway, to link it back to the house. Not only did this tie the two buildings together but it also created a wonderful courtyard on the south side of the house. This area is further subdivided by a low wall just over 3ft/1m high that reinforces a slight change of level, and keeps the more public space outside the front door apart from the private space by the sitting room. The latter area – a terrace sheltered by walls, surrounded by scented planting and

fronting a small lawn – is the quietest and most intimate part of the garden. We breakfast here and can sit in the sun until lunch, by which time the whole of the main garden is in sun. In the afternoon and evening, the sheltered terrace outside the kitchen comes into its own. Here, there is a built-in barbecue, raised beds, plenty of room for entertaining, and access through wide French doors to the kitchen.

Beyond this terrace, a brick path from the gate leads the eyes – and the feet – to an ornamental pool with a bubble jet, set against the wall of the barn. The pool is fed by an artificial stream with a rocky floor, planted with a wide range of water-side species, that runs alongside the path. The stream itself is fed by a waterfall, a feature that provides the main focal point from the kitchen and terrace; water slides from an upper pool, drops 3ft/1m, and strikes carefully positioned

Left This Kugel or water globe, like the one on my sitting-room terrace, is a perfect example of a beautifully thought-out and constructed focal point. The ball is a solid sphere of granite and floats on very low-pressure jets of water in a precision-engineered cup.

Opposite I find water, in all its many moods, compelling, and particularly prize its power and movement – qualities I can maximize on a sloping site. Design possibilities are endless: in this futuristic water feature, I used mirrored pools.

large stones before flowing downstream.

From here, the garden rises up in a series of rectangular terraces. Broad steps climb past the waterfall to a stone-paved landing, where a seat flanked by two *Prunus serrula* looks across the long reflective pool and its wall fountain to two old fruit trees.

Moving on up, a gravel path partly covered by a pergola surrounds a spacious lawn. A paved area leads out to the garage forecourt. The planting plan here is presently being developed. It involves an informal copse of largely indigenous trees to screen the drive, which will flow into more controlled drifts of shrubs, hardy perennials, and grasses. Tall modern shrub roses will screen the garage and bamboos hide the boiler house. Vines will clothe all the walls, linking building, and landscape.

At the end of the day, I see the garden as an evolving pattern, and as a designer I shall most certainly change the planting over the years to reflect my current thinking. A garden, like its owner, can never be static; it must change to embrace new ideas, criteria, and materials.

A mountain garden

The creation of a garden depends on molding the spaces to a particular set of requirements, and shaping a composition to bind house and environment together so that the one flows naturally into the other. The architect Julian Elliott and his wife Helene have done this successfully with their garden set on the slopes of Table Mountain, in South Africa.

They had a head start in that they started from scratch. The only "given features" when they came to the site were the stream, with its large brick pipe, its canalization, and stone bed, a number of mature trees, and various smaller plants. More, they had a goal: "House and garden," says Julian Elliott, "are part of a long search for ways of integrating and creating a sense of unity between the interior and exterior

Opposite Water is a dynamic element in this garden, running freely over rounded natural boulders and surrounded by lush ferns, acanthus, nasturtiums, monsteras, and arum lilies.

Below The plan shows the integration of hard and soft landscape, with different surfaces interacting and pushing out over the stream into the wider garden.

Key to planting areas

1 Ground cover planting with ferns and impatiens

2 Ferns and mondo grass

3 Natural planting with ground cover, ferns, acanthus, and eugenia

4 Heavily planted bank with acanthus, nasturtiums, bougainvillea, impatiens, bamboo, and mondo grass

5 Bank planted with morning glory and wild cannas and ground cover of periwinkles, ivy, and wandering Jew

6 Lush planting with monsteras and nandinas

7 Mound of mondo grass

8 Bamboo grove with moonflowers and cannas

9 Informal garden with azaleas, japonicas, moonflowers, ferns, and mondo grass

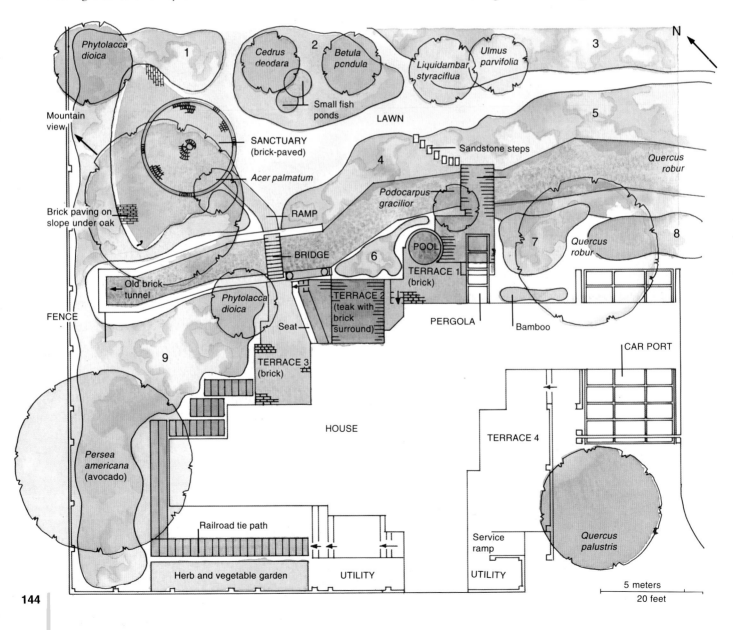

environments." At the same time as expressing a "seamless" unity, the interior and exterior realms were to retain their integrity: here, transitional spaces, pergolas, awnings, terraces, and the hard landscaping played a major role.

The house and garden are refreshingly contemporary, but while this environment could only have been created in the late twentieth century it incorporates ideas and memories from other places and other times. There are clear influences of California, the Mediterranean, and Japan, small fragments of the Moorish Paradise garden, and, less obvious but equally important, the influence of Africa, where a dominant courtyard often surrounds a central enclosed living core.

This core – the house – has a linear pattern, stepping up with the contours of the sloping site. It opens out onto the garden at many points, particularly on the sunny northern side. Here, a series of terraces, built with a combination of teak decking and brick paving, similarly follow the changing ground level; each terrace provides ample room to sit, dine, and entertain.

The character of the terraces is strongly architectural, but they are planted in such a way that this crisp outline is immediately tempered by the lush vegetation that thrives in the deep fertile soil and moist climate. Such planting relies on the rich texture and shape of foliage rather than flower color for its effect, an approach that provides interest over much of the year and one that takes its cue from the Elliotts' interest in Japan.

A stream that runs through the garden and tumbles down

Above The magical atmosphere of the brick-paved sanctuary is formed by its restful circular shape cut into the slope and the enclosing screen of architectural planting.

Right The teak-decked terrace is one of three that exploit the sunny side of the house, and act as transitional spaces. Steps and a built-in seat, bounded by a red polished-granite waterslide, rise to a brick terrace and wooden bridge that leads to the sanctuary and the garden beyond.

the steeply changing levels is an integral part of the design. Two bridges cross the water, the larger of the two extending the line of the deck that surrounds the circular pool. The stream, with its boisterous movement and soothing background sound, provides a natural division between the immediate living areas close to the house and the wilder garden beyond. There, the design is altogether more relaxed, with the emphasis on the fluid shapes of planting and lawn that run with the contours.

The edges of the garden are thickly planted, especially toward the north in order to provide shelter from the harsh winter winds and to screen neighboring buildings. This gives a firm feeling of enclosure, though to the west there are glimpses of beautiful views of the mountainside.

Like all the best gardens, there is a secret place for sitting, just visible from the house but partially hidden, so that it offers a feeling of mystery and surprise – elements that will naturally draw you toward it. The Elliotts call this part of the garden the "sanctuary," an ideal spot for relaxing, away from the inevitably busier areas around the house. The circular shape provides a feeling of intimacy, while the surrounding planting gives shade and shelter.

The older trees, including oak, avocado, and belombra (*Phytolacca dioica*), which were part of the original site, have all been preserved, and to these have been added a number of more decorative species such as liquidambar, cedar, Japanese maple, bamboo, and monstera, which add interest primarily by their foliage, overall shape, or texture of bark.

Above Nasturtiums, acanthus, and bougainvillea bring touches of flower color to the rich foliage-dominant planting.

Left The lowest terrace with the pool is shaded by a pergola and a graceful *Afrocarpus gracilior* (*Podocarpus g.*). The teak deck extends the line of the house into the garden.

A stroll garden

Some of the most satisfying garden designs are born not of a wealth of design experience but rather from a sensitive understanding of the site, combined with a clear objective.

When Yvon-Serge Lesné moved home, some years ago, he was looking for a town house of ample size to hold his growing art and furniture collection. The house he found was a traditional *maison bourgeoise,* built at the end of the nineteenth century, spacious, well-proportioned – and derelict. The façade giving onto the boulevard was in granite, at the back the walls were concrete, with granite window surrounds. Behind it was an overgrown garden of an interesting irregular shape, surrounded by five stone

Below This irregularly shaped plot, sheltered by walls and surrounded by buildings, has been divided into a series of individual garden rooms. The finished composition is a delicate balance of hard and soft landscape, the one complementing the other.

Opposite The terrace, floored with Belgian blocks and surrounded by luxuriant planting, makes a charmingly intimate dining room. The planting, which screens the terrace from the rest of the garden, is a combination of shrubs and herbaceous plants that is largely geared to summer interest and fragrance.

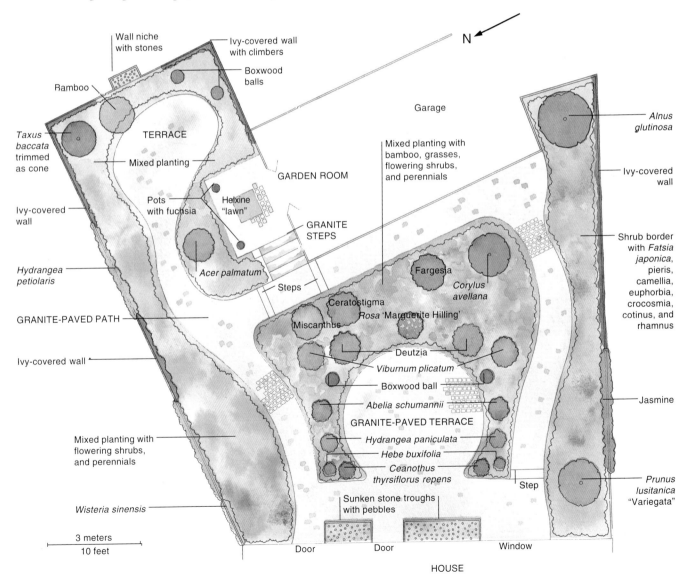

Wall niche with stones

Ivy-covered wall with climbers

Boxwood balls

Bamboo

N

Garage

Taxus baccata trimmed as cone

TERRACE

Mixed planting

GARDEN ROOM

Mixed planting with bamboo, grasses, flowering shrubs, and perennials

Alnus glutinosa

Ivy-covered wall

Ivy-covered wall

Pots with fuchsia

Helxine "lawn"

GRANITE STEPS

Shrub border with *Fatsia japonica,* pieris, camellia, euphorbia, crocosmia, cotinus, and rhamnus

Hydrangea petiolaris

Acer palmatum

Steps

Fargesia

Corylus avellana

Ceratostigma

Rosa 'Marguerite Hilling'

GRANITE-PAVED PATH

Miscanthus

Deutzia

Viburnum plicatum

Ivy-covered wall

Boxwood ball

Abelia schumannii

Jasmine

GRANITE-PAVED TERRACE

Mixed planting with flowering shrubs, and perennials

Hydrangea paniculata

Hebe buxifolia

Ceanothus thyrsiflorus repens

Step

Prunus lusitanica "Variegata"

Wisteria sinensis

3 meters
10 feet

Sunken stone troughs with pebbles

Door

Door

Window

HOUSE

walls of the local Brittany granite, and with the bonus of an old coach house at the far end.

Lesné supervised the extensive work on the house himself, opening up the back wall with a large picture window, which increased his enjoyment of the garden outside. He also put a big glass door in the wall of the coach house that gives onto the helxine-covered courtyard. However, he realized he needed help with the garden and asked Timothy Vaughan, an Englishman who had moved to Brittany to start a tree nursery, to carry out the design. It was Vaughan's first project, and he undertook it with great enthusiasm. Lesné's only stipulation was that there should be a terrace plus lots of other paving, all to be built from the local Belgian blocks.

Vaughan's design is fluid in outline and is built up from a series of paths that subdivide the garden into a number of individual rooms. The main terrace, which is close to the house, is circular, and its shape is emphasized by round boxwood balls that define the space and punctuate the rich mix of shrubs and herbaceous plants surrounding the area. To the left, a long path meanders down to a second, secret, terrace, an outdoor sitting room much used for reading and resting. Here again, the terrace is surrounded by plants, which screen it from the charming sunken garden, carpeted with helxine, that leads out from the renovated coach house.

The framework of paths allows you to stroll and to become intimately involved with both Lesné's collection of garden ornaments and Vaughan's planting. This planting is an interesting combination of unusual species and more common varieties that shows off both to the best effect. Deliciously subtle, this is the composition of a plantsman rather than the broad swaths of a landscape architect, and makes of this series of outdoor rooms an ever-changing source of fascination and delight.

Opposite left Simple but elegant stone steps, softened by a self-seeded planting of helxine, lead down to the sunken garden that adjoins the old coach house.

Opposite right A carpet of helxine, in the sunken garden. Helxine is a rampant spreader but is kept in check here by the surrounding path of Belgian blocks. The pots, planted with fuchsias, add focus and interest, while plants soften the retaining walls and cast shadows across the lawn – a welcome relief in hot weather when the coach house is used for dining.

Above The paths running throughout this garden serve a variety of useful purposes. As well as subdividing the space, they are ideal for strolling and chatting. Because the paths meander, you walk a long way in relation to the size of the garden, thus making the area feel larger than it really is. They also simplify maintenance of the planting. The blocks used for surfacing throughout the garden are here allowed to merge into the beds, the plants flopping out over either side. The fascinating mix of colors and textures reveals a plantsman's hand and eye.

A flower arranger's garden

Gardens, like people, change and develop with age and often have to conform to a succession of quite different lifestyles. It is a designer's job to accommodate any such changes, while retaining worthwhile features that remain in tune with the owner's needs.

The original scheme for this Los Angeles garden was created in the 1960's by Garrett Eckbo, one of the leading garden designers of the twentieth century. Eckbo, a pioneer of the outdoor room, produced a garden that was admirably suited to the needs of a young family, and to the hot climate of southern California. Ample room was provided for sitting and dining, with a broad yellow brick terrace directly outside the sliding doors of the main living area forming a clear link between inside and out. The yellow brick echoes that used in parts of the house for flooring, and this reinforces the bond between architecture and landscape.

Shade is an important requirement in this part of the world, and to the left of the main terrace Eckbo created a shady bower, roofed by a pergola smothered with vines.

The remainder of the plot slopes gently down away from the house. This area was largely given over to lawn, for play, with a dramatic planting of *Ficus benjamina* framing the grass

Above right Though the planting in the raised beds is remarkably varied in height, form, and texture, there is a sense of unity, achieved by arranging individual plants in color bands. Here, roses, foxgloves, dianthus, and geraniums combine in a medley of pinks, purples, and white. The broken concrete walls are clearly visible, but softened by plants that tumble from level to level.

Right The original garden followed a strongly conceived but essentially simple design. Chris Rosmini has taken the outline as a starting point and overlaid it with a series of richly planted terraces that work their way down to the lawn (**opposite**). Sight lines have been carefully considered, the arbor at the end of the garden being skillfully positioned to terminate the view.

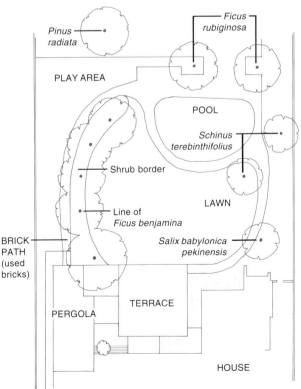

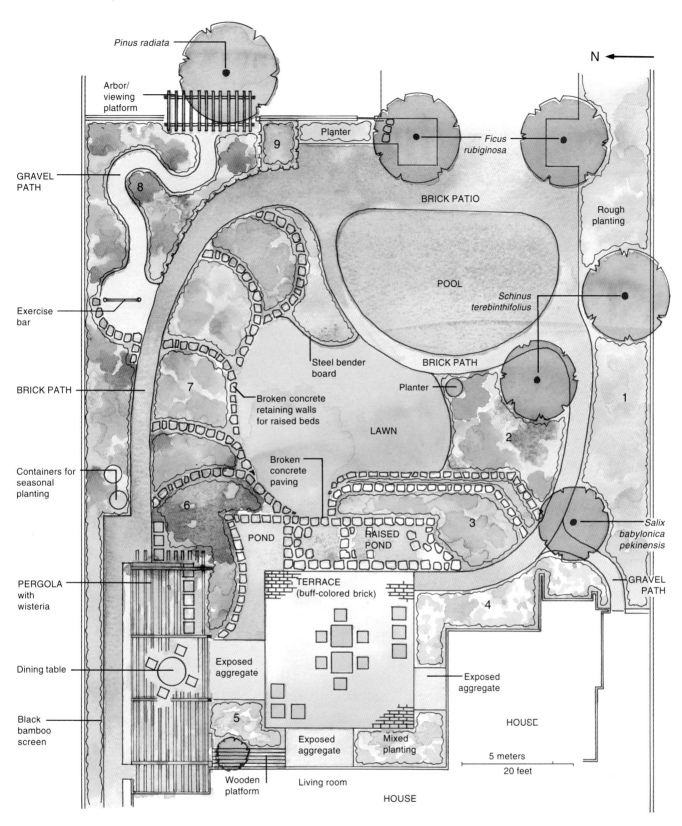

Pinus radiata

Arbor/
viewing
platform

GRAVEL
PATH

Exercise
bar

BRICK PATH

Containers for
seasonal
planting

PERGOLA
with
wisteria

Dining table

Black
bamboo
screen

9

8

7

6

POND

Steel bender
board

Broken concrete
retaining walls
for raised beds

Broken
concrete
paving

Planter

BRICK PATIO

Ficus
rubiginosa

Rough
planting

POOL

Schinus
terebinthifolius

BRICK PATH

Planter

LAWN

RAISED
POND

3

2

1

Salix
babylonica
pekinensis

GRAVEL
PATH

4

TERRACE
(buff-colored brick)

Exposed
aggregate

Exposed
aggregate

5

Mixed
planting

HOUSE

Exposed
aggregate

Wooden
platform

Living room

HOUSE

N

5 meters

20 feet

1 Shade planting with azaleas, camellias, hydrangeas, and ferns

2 Part shade planting with flowering shrubs and perennials, including *Clerodendrum myricoides* "Ugandense," *Helleborus* spp., and *Cyclamen* spp. under tree

3 Raised beds with peach-colored small cannas, pastel eschscholzia, *Scaevola* "Mauve Clusters," and

Digitalis "Sutton's Apricot"

4 Variegated and white flowers with dwarf white agapanthus, astilbe, *Clerodendrum bungei*, variegated grasses, and *Pileostegia viburnoides* on wall

5 Japanese garden with crape myrtle, azaleas, dwarf mondo grass, and white clematis on bamboo frame

6 Mixed planting with *Homeria ochroleuca*, *Heliotropium arborescens*, *Dianella* spp., and *Miscanthus sinensis* "Zebrinus" near pond

7 Raised beds with gray foliage and salmon, pink, and lavender flowering plants including watsonia, *Alstroemeria* Meyer hybrids, *Limonium perezii*, and pelargoniums

8 Mixed planting in hot colors including *Cosmos atrosanguineus*, Garnette roses, bronze-leaf cannas

9 Mixed planting in yellows and grays including *Verbascum bombyciferum*, *Artemisia* "Powis Castle," and a winter-blooming pair *Euphorbia rigida* and *Tulbaghia fragrans*

Left The shelter of a pergola creates a softly enclosed and private outdoor room, a haven of dappled shade, where the owners can dine, entertain guests, or simply sit and look over the garden to the more distant landscape, framed by trees. An exercise bar for early morning or evening workouts has been integrated into the design.

Above As well as enriching the planting, Rosmini added a split-level pool that acts as a link between the hard landscaping of the terrace and the soft planting beyond. This pool not only provides a home for lilies and other aquatic plants but also adds the movement of reflections, and of the water bubbling through the simple jet. Already existing trees make an effective backdrop, giving shelter and privacy. In the planting around the pool, the emphasis is on leaf shape and texture – iris and grasses contributing strong vertical lines – while, here as throughout the garden, pots are used to add instant interest and color.

Above The mellow paving bricks of the terrace run away from the house and out into the garden. Pots and planting soften the space, and the simple furniture has been well-chosen to complement the terrace design. Cream is a good color for bright sun.

on the north side. The swimming pool at the bottom of the garden was added in the 1970's.

By the 1980's, the family was at a different stage. The owner, now her children were grown-up, had more time to enjoy her interest in gardening and in flower arranging. In 1985, Chris Rosmini was asked to adapt Eckbo's very workable space into a garden that placed greater emphasis on planting. A major structural change was the removal of the line of *Ficus benjamina*, gross feeders which had drained the surrounding area of nourishment. These were the only trees taken out, the remainder being worked into the composition. All the hard landscaping close to the house was retained, but with the addition of a split-level pool. Water provides another dimension, with its reflections and sound

adding to the overall enjoyment of the area.

It was agreed that the size of the lawn should be reduced to make room for a series of raised beds that work their way down the changing levels. This alteration increases the feeling of movement and space. The end of the garden was contoured to match the ground level near the house. Thus sitting on the lawn surrounded by planting at a higher level feels rather like sitting in a bowl of flowers.

Because there is little suitable local stone, Rosmini used broken concrete as the main material in the construction of both retaining walls and paving. This is an excellent example of sensible recycling. If the quality of the concrete is good, the exposed edges look not unlike dressed stone, the soft gray providing an ideal backdrop for planting.

Beyond and to the left of the swimming pool, Rosmini sited an arbor and viewing platform to act as a focal point and visual full stop when looking from the house. The view back from here is a delightful one, taking in the ascending layers of planting as they rise toward the building.

Because the owner wanted to have a wide choice of

Above The end of the garden is informal, with a gravel path leading through a loose planting of roses, pelargoniums, and watsonia to the arbor over the viewing platform. This, together with the mature tree, acts as a focal point and punctuates the view. Plain wooden furniture echoes the solidity of the hand rail. A seemingly casual arrangement of hard and soft features conceals subtle control of a carefully thought-out design.

Opposite Framed by a shady tree, the swimming pool sweeps in a strong curve. The line of this pool, one of the dominant features of the garden, is echoed in the shape of the new lawn and the terraced beds that climb back toward the house. The backdrop of planting around the pool helps to soften both the geometric line and the view across the arbor and the informal sitting area.

Baskets hanging from the tree branches are an inspired thought.

flowers for cutting and arranging, the planting includes as many different species and varieties as possible. The danger of such an approach is that the overall design can look very busy. To counter this and provide visual continuity, plants have been arranged here by color themes. Planting in color bands also makes it easier for the owner to locate particular plants for cutting. The coloring, taking its initial cue from the mauve wisteria planted over the pergola close to the house, moves from purple, pink, and salmon to soft yellows and grays toward the bottom of the garden. The composition is essentially built up from pastel hues. A strong color grouping of hot reds and yellows is positioned at the bottom of the garden, but this has been screened from the house by climbing plants growing up arches made of copper irrigation pipes in the terraced beds.

Overall, this garden shows a sensitive manipulation of the original plan into an altogether softer design, a trend that is apparent in many contemporary North American gardens.

A garden oasis

People often think of formal gardens simply in historical terms, yet some of the most unusual and innovative contemporary gardens are unashamedly formal in both character and outline.

This garden, in a small but bustling town in northern Flanders, is small and nearly square, measuring 52x40ft/ 16x12m. This is an uncompromising shape, and the designer Jacques Wirtz dealt with it in uncompromising fashion, fitting within it a strictly geometrical circular pattern.

The garden was primarily intended to be a haven, a place to withdraw away from the demands of a busy life. Although the walled boundaries provided shelter and a degree of privacy, it was considered essential to increase their height. This was achieved by extending trellis above the brickwork. The pierced outline is less oppressive than brick, and the perfect host for a range of climbing plants that will in time shield the garden completely.

In this peaceful oasis, water is an essential element. A

Above The main axis of the garden is defined by the narrow pool and fountains and terminates at the seat, flanked by trees, that acts as the principal focal point. The trellis provides ample screening, while allowing the sun to filter between the tracery of vines. The differing heights of the hedges, perfectly trimmed, reinforce the geometry of the design.

Left From a point off-center of the axis, the powerful rhythm of the circular pattern becomes apparent. The circular theme, marked by the strong curves of the cobbled path and the pool, is echoed in the hedges, where the rounded tops of boxwood balls emphasize niches that house garden ornaments.

Opposite The success of this design lies in its formality and symmetry.

The circular pattern, delineated by water, paving, and formal planting, is restful and stable, while at the same time encouraging movement through the space.

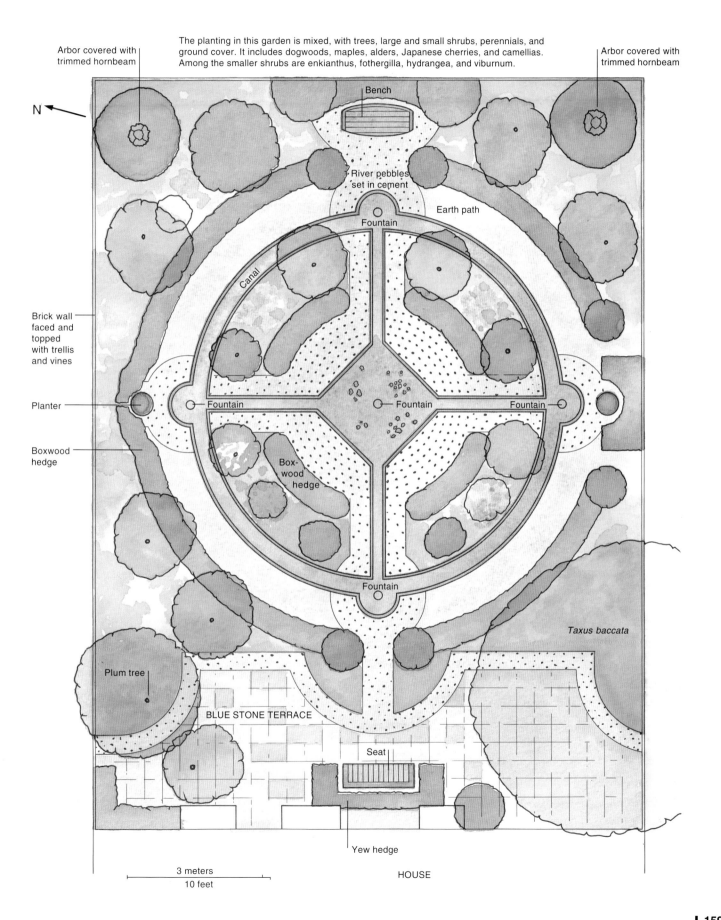

Arbor covered with trimmed hornbeam

The planting in this garden is mixed, with trees, large and small shrubs, perennials, and ground cover. It includes dogwoods, maples, alders, Japanese cherries, and camellias. Among the smaller shrubs are enkianthus, fothergilla, hydrangea, and viburnum.

Arbor covered with trimmed hornbeam

Bench

N

River pebbles set in cement

Fountain

Earth path

Canal

Brick wall faced and topped with trellis and vines

Planter

Fountain

Fountain

Fountain

Boxwood hedge

Box-wood hedge

Fountain

Taxus baccata

Plum tree

BLUE STONE TERRACE

Seat

3 meters

10 feet

Yew hedge

HOUSE

159

Left Backed by vines and surrounded by enclosing hedges, the seat at the end of the garden provides a secluded retreat. From here, you look back across the whole garden toward the house.

The subtle variation in the cobbles is brought out when they are wet, and then the intricate patterning becomes more obvious.

Opposite Viewed from the first-floor terrace, the circular pattern, emphasized by the placing of the cobbles and the planting, is thrown into sharp relief. The hedges provide evergreen space division that is even more telling in winter.

circular canal is divided by a cruciform shape that sets up the main cross-axis of the garden. In the center, the water opens up into a square pool surrounded by a low boxwood hedge, which is reflected by a higher hedge outside the canal, reinforcing a sense of intimacy and enclosure. Four fountains, one at either end of each of the rills that make up the central cross, provide movement and sound, helping to distract from the noise of traffic outside the garden.

For geometry to be effective in a garden, the shapes must be simple and clear-cut, and interact to make a workable and comfortable space. The strength of this garden lies in the way all the parts work smoothly together. The floor, beautifully laid in small closely packed cobbles, is a study in careful detailing. Its patterns reflect the overall shape of the garden, sweeping around the central pool and fountains in a series of circles, while the edges of the pools are picked out in sharp relief by rounded concrete edging. Like most natural materials, the cobbles change color when they are wet, the polished surfaces sparkling and individual stones contrasting with one another.

The planting is restrained, being essentially shrubs and trees. Where smaller species are used as ground cover, they are grouped in bold drifts that provide continuity and give added strength to the overall composition.

A narrow urban garden

A clever and imaginative rethink transformed a long, narrow featureless urban plot (outlined in the plan on the right) into the perfect series of outdoor rooms shown in the photograph opposite.

The site is typical of many in an urban setting, measuring about 25x100ft/7.5x30m. Before it was redesigned by Christopher Masson, it suffered from a lack of overall plan, with features such as rose beds, greenhouse, and a raised concrete pool placed seemingly at random. A long straight path and narrow borders accentuated the garden's lack of width just as vertically striped wallpaper makes a tall room look even taller. The original layout simply accelerated the view down the garden, foreshortening the space and failing to exploit its potential.

The sun swings off the back of the house relatively early in the day. This, plus the fact that there is a steep change in level where the ground is stepped up close to the house, meant that the area immediately next to it seemed cramped and uncomfortable as well as being in shade for most of the day. It therefore offered little incentive to go out and use the garden.

Apart from the rather attractive remains of an early nineteenth-century wall and a few trees that were clearly worth preserving, most of the garden required a drastic overhaul if its owner was to get the most out of it.

Beautiful as well as functional, the redesigned garden fulfils Masson's requirements: not only does it now have a coherent structure that divides it into a number of attractive and functional rooms, thanks to clever landscaping it appears larger and wider than it actually is. A wooden deck with overheads for shade-giving climbing plants catches the early morning sun, and is a perfect spot for breakfasting. This small deck gives onto the area next to the house, which is opened up into an attractively paved terrace for sitting, dining, and entertaining. Foliage helps soften the general architectural feel of this area, which takes its cue from the adjoining house. Brick steps link the garden and terrace with the lower paved area and form a visual link with the old garden wall.

Broad steps that run virtually the full width of the garden

Below The starting point is shown in this plan of the garden before Christopher Masson redesigned it and fully exploited its potential. An uninteresting narrow rectangle, with a few trees and randomly placed outbuildings, it invited neither use nor exploration. There was an awkward change of level close to the house, and planting was limited to long narrow borders against the boundaries and island beds.

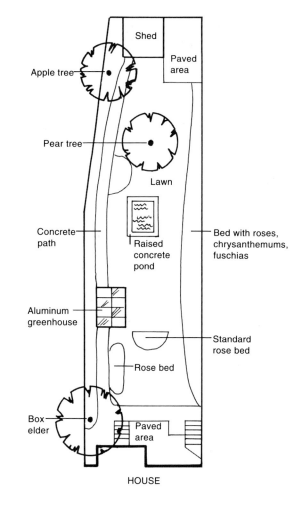

Opposite The redesigned garden is a place to enjoy. It is possible to move from one space to another with a feeling of mystery and surprise. Various levels and areas relate comfortably, and the long lines of paving and grass set across the space create a feeling of greater width. This is essentially a formal layout, with architectural planting and garden structures positioned to give the design strength of purpose.

define the terrace boundary, and their positive line is reinforced by a wide band of paving bricks that also serves to make the area appear wider.

Trimmed boxwood cubes direct the eyes and feet either across the lawn and beneath the pergola that frames the view to more distant parts of the garden or to the sitting area near the pond.

This central area is full of interest and pivots around the intriguing pools that are linked by a channel beneath the lawn.

Right Water is used as a transitional element between the soft lawn and the hard paved area around the summerhouse. Its limpid reflective qualities link it with the surrounding planting, and it also acts as a gentle foil to the underlying geometry of the design. The flow of water in the pond is kept to a minimum to retain the feeling of calm engendered by the garden.

Right A tiny leafy bower next to the pond is as suited to quiet contemplation as to conversation. Four individual seat units look out over the lawn, guiding the eye across the garden and reinforcing the impression of width.

Being able to sit in various parts of the garden at different times adds to the overall impression of space.

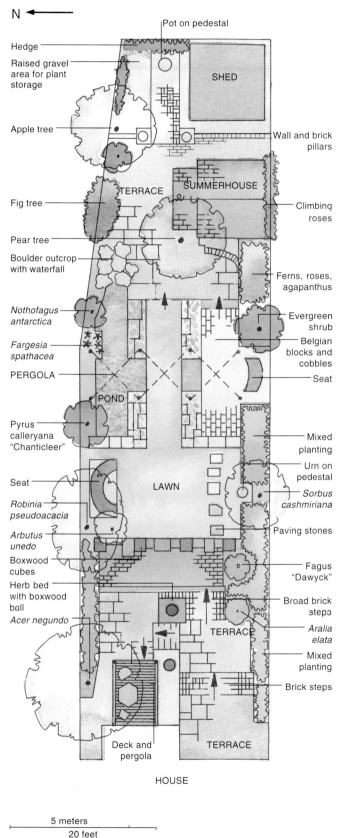

N ←

Hedge
Raised gravel area for plant storage
Apple tree
Pot on pedestal
SHED
Wall and brick pillars
TERRACE
SUMMERHOUSE
Fig tree
Climbing roses
Pear tree
Boulder outcrop with waterfall
Ferns, roses, agapanthus
Nothofagus antarctica
Evergreen shrub
Fargesia spathacea
Belgian blocks and cobbles
PERGOLA
Seat
POND
Mixed planting
Pyrus calleryana "Chanticleer"
Urn on pedestal
Sorbus cashmiriana
Seat
LAWN
Robinia pseudoacacia
Paving stones
Arbutus unedo
Boxwood cubes
Herb bed with boxwood ball
Acer negundo
Fagus "Dawyck"
Broad brick steps
Aralia elata
Mixed planting
TERRACE
Brick steps
Deck and pergola
TERRACE
HOUSE

5 meters
20 feet

Left The metamorphosis is clear and successful. The new plan has a purposeful structure that marries hard and soft landscapes in a design that makes maximum use of the space available. The beauty of this design lies in its subdivision of space: each area has its own character, which subtly draws you onto the next. It is also slightly unusual in that it moves from a strongly architectural area near the house, through the softly framed lawn, and then onto another well-defined space by the summerhouse. Thus there is a rhythmic movement and an overall feeling of stability as the composition returns to a structured form.

Above An enticing site in a "secret" area toward the end of the garden is the obvious spot for a beautifully constructed summerhouse. Sunlight filters in all day during the summer, and in late afternoon the sun bounces light in from the pond. A lush mantle of planting softens the area around it.

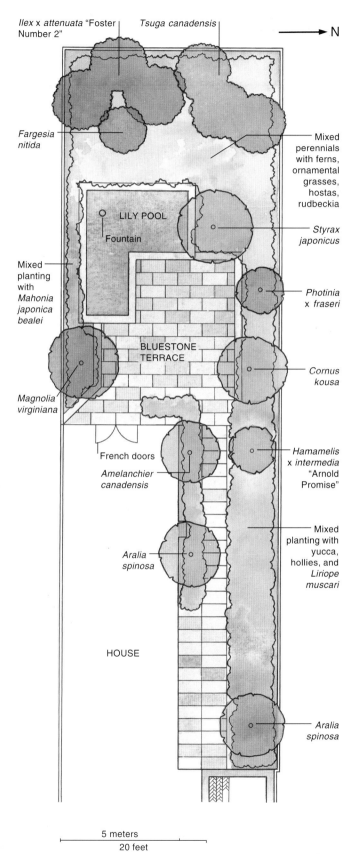

Ilex x attenuata "Foster Number 2"

Tsuga canadensis

→ N

Fargesia nitida

Mixed perennials with ferns, ornamental grasses, hostas, rudbeckia

LILY POOL

Fountain

Styrax japonicus

Mixed planting with *Mahonia japonica bealei*

Photinia x *fraseri*

BLUESTONE TERRACE

Cornus kousa

Magnolia virginiana

French doors

Amelanchier canadensis

Hamamelis x *intermedia* "Arnold Promise"

Mixed planting with yucca, hollies, and *Liriope muscari*

Aralia spinosa

HOUSE

Aralia spinosa

5 meters
20 feet

A small city garden

One basic design criterion states that the smaller the garden the more difficult it is to create a worthwhile and workable composition. In part this is due to size constraints that are in direct opposition to the number of features that may need to be incorporated. The answer, as this design shows, is to keep it simple. This garden is indeed small, the main area, to the rear of the house, being barely 30ft/9m wide and only 50ft/15m long. At the side of the house is a pathway with planted borders. The house is close to its neighbors, and there is a need for privacy on all the boundaries.

The owners, keen gardeners, also wanted a pleasant place to entertain and relax. To meet their needs and aesthetic preferences they chose as designers James van Sweden and Wolfgang Oehme, pioneers in an exciting modern American style of garden design, brilliantly exemplified here. This is an all-seasons approach in which it is vital that architectural and evergreen backbone planting look good year-round. The planting relies on trees, shrubs, bulbs, and perennials, emphasizing native American plants and grasses. Water is an essential feature, and the unity of the house and garden is important, with one complementing and leading out of the other.

The layout of the house in relation to the garden was influenced by this design, and a dining room and upstairs bedroom, with a balcony overlooking the garden, were added to the house. Wide doors from the dining room lead

Left The plan shows the simplicity of the design. It consists of three elements: two – the terrace and the raised lily pond – are bold rectangular shapes softened by the third, the planting. The pool and the paving make the central area seem light, while the planting around the periphery lends privacy.

Opposite Looking back toward the house reveals how the rectangular shapes of pool and paving fit together, creating rhythm and balance. The angular line of the pool continues as a raised bed to the house, while on the other side the paving angles around the house, becoming a path to the street gate.

directly out onto a stone terrace, of ample size for relaxing or entertaining, which wraps itself around the building giving access to the side and front of the property.

The natural blue-stone paving stones are laid with a staggered bond *across* the space, and these long lines help to increase the sensation of width. Screening in a small garden should always be as straightforward as possible, and the fences here are built from simple gray vertical slats, butted together so that there is total privacy. This neutral color is unobtrusive and an excellent foil for the planting that breaks and softens the outline. The raised pool is also built and coped in natural stone, providing a link with the terrace. The major garden feature, both from inside and outside the house, it introduces

movement and reflections through every season of the year. Its simple shape helps to balance the mass of the paved area, and it is set at an easy height for sitting. The line of the pool is carried on at the same height around the garden, and a raised bed is formed behind it.

The planting is a well-chosen combination of largely evergreen structure plants, which give the composition mass and form, and lighter, more colorful material that provides brighter tones and seasonal interest. It is fascinating to see the character of the garden change from spring to summer – the tall line of the tulips bring welcome early color, while the lusher foliage of grasses and shrubs, interspersed with hardy perennials, fill the borders during summer.

Opposite An overview of the garden in high summer reveals the beauty of the execution of the plan. The cool blues and grays of the natural stone balance the greens of the plants and the dark reflective pool.

The planting is a marvelous juxtaposition of forms, shape, and texture, punctuated by vibrant notes of bright color. For example, in one corner there are the graceful plumes of grasses – pennisetum in front of the pool, miscanthus behind – the spikes of yucca, arrow-shaped sagittaria leaves, and a canopy of *Styrax japonicus* overhead. Red hibiscus, a pot of columnea, and yellow rudbeckia and ligularia add bright color accents.

Left There is a smooth transition between house and garden. The open doors of the dining room welcome the viewer into the garden, with the pool providing the major focal point. The low walls provide attractive bench seating and add interesting changes of level.

Above Pink and white lily-flowered tulips brighten the pool surround in spring, contrasting with the dark line of *Mahonia japonica bealei* along the far side. Feathery spikes of *Typha angustifolia* rise from the bright water, which is edged by the soft dark shadow of the neatly laid overhanging copestones.

A terraced garden

The owner of this garden is passionate about it, works long and hard on it – and the end result is spectacular and highly original. Like many garden owners, she found the bones of the garden already there when she took it over, and her time has been spent not on major structural reorganization but in something quite as radical – changing the entire look and feel of the space through the planting.

The plot, in New South Wales, Australia, is approximately 140ft/43m long and 65ft/20m wide, set on a steeply sloping site that drops some 60ft/18m from the front to a creek at the back. The house was built in the 1920's, and the garden layout was conceived by the architect, who naturally terraced the slope, incorporating retaining walls, steps, and paths to rationalize the drastic changes in level. The original planting design was flower-filled, emphasizing pastel colors, particularly mauve, reflecting the fashion of the time for annuals.

In stark contrast, the present owner has fashioned an all-seasons garden from trees, shrubs, and perennials. In it, excitement, beauty, and diversity lie in the manipulation of the shapes, size, texture, and foliage of the various plants rather than in flower color. If one color is important above all others it is green, in its vast range of shades and tones. The owner is fascinated by different plant forms and leaf shapes, and she uses and juxtaposes them in an instinctive and masterly way. Throughout the garden there are examples of planting – massive trimmed gardenias and neat little boxwood balls, spiky iris leaves, variegated euonymus, fleshy rosettes of succulents, undulating leaves of zantedeschia – that create satisfying contrast and interest year-round.

The planting is dense but not unruly, as it is set in a highly

Right The plan shows how well the original terracing of the steep site has been exploited to create separate garden areas that divide the rather long narrow plot. The potentially awkward triangular space for the front garden has been beautifully treated with formal lines and curves that create a rhythmical pattern.

At the back of the house, a narrow flag terrace looks out over attractively planted raised beds and steps leading down to a spacious rectangular lawn, bordered by formal hedges. Steps in the corner lead through the wild garden, which is thickly planted with native trees and tree ferns, to the creek below.

Opposite The sloping lawns of the front garden are edged with low hedges of boxwood. Flowing curves against the fence surround specimen plants such as trimmed boxwood balls, gardenias, and an urn planted with succulents. Tall trimmed camellias on the opposite side add height, and the whole creates a rhythmical balanced picture.

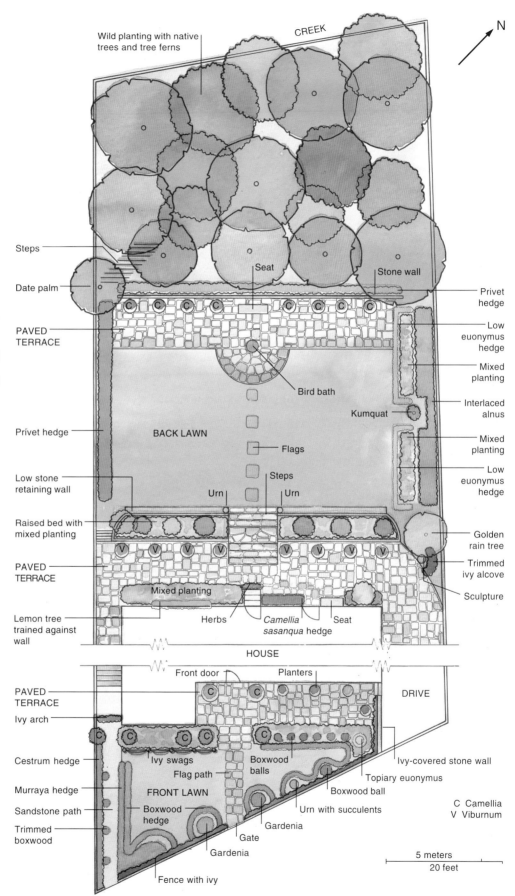

N

CREEK

Wild planting with native trees and tree ferns

Steps

Date palm

Seat

Stone wall

PAVED TERRACE

Privet hedge

Low euonymus hedge

Mixed planting

Interlaced alnus

Bird bath

Kumquat

Mixed planting

Privet hedge

BACK LAWN

Low euonymus hedge

Low stone retaining wall

Flags

Steps

Raised bed with mixed planting

Urn

Urn

Golden rain tree

Trimmed ivy alcove

PAVED TERRACE

Sculpture

Mixed planting

Lemon tree trained against wall

Herbs

Camellia sasanqua hedge

Seat

HOUSE

Front door

Planters

PAVED TERRACE

DRIVE

Ivy arch

Cestrum hedge

Ivy swags

Boxwood balls

Ivy-covered stone wall

Murraya hedge

Flag path

Topiary euonymus

Boxwood ball

Sandstone path

FRONT LAWN

Urn with succulents

Trimmed boxwood

Boxwood hedge

Gardenia

C Camellia
V Viburnum

Gate

Gardenia

5 meters
20 feet

Fence with ivy

Opposite An overview of the front garden shows how effectively the design relies on form and the subtle juxtaposition of different layers and shades of green to make a satisfying composition. The rounded forms of the trimmed gardenias, tiered euonymus, and neat little boxwood balls contrast with the lines and planes of the hedges and lawns.

Left Self-seeded plants soften the mellow stone steps leading down from the terrace at the back of the house. At the bottom they are flanked by two *Cordyline australis* in elegant urns. At the top is a herb garden in pots, and a lemon tree trained against the house wall.

Below The view from the back terrace toward the bottom of the garden reveals a balanced design. Flags mark the central axis crossing the lawn to a decorative bird bath and stone seat, flanked by trimmed camellias in pots.

formal structure with a rich use of topiary. Hedges and specimen plants are all sheared into neat solid shapes, and the lawns are closely mown. In fact, the garden needs constant cutting back, owing to the prolific plant growth rate caused by the climate, irrigation, and the rich soil – originally all-but-unworkable clay, now much improved by the owner's constant mulching and fertilizing. There is one completely wild area at the back, which descends sharply to the creek below, offering a lovely contrast to the contained, structured garden that surrounds the house.

Because the site itself is so dramatic, the owner's overriding aim is and has been to get the scale and perspective of the planting right. This involves both having a ground plan that is satisfying to look at from above – which the balanced and shapely formal design achieves – and having a number of eye-catching vistas throughout the garden, each with an attractive focal point such as an urn, a pot, or a specimen plant; ideally, she thinks there should be such a view from each house window. In this garden, every element contributes to the overall composition, and each is set with great care and precision.

A walled garden

Shelter is one of the greatest assets a garden can have. When Mark Rumary acquired Magnolia House, an eighteenth-century house in an East Anglian village, in England, he was delighted by the possibilities of the garden. Hidden away behind the house and backing onto parkland, it was enclosed by high brick walls, with a screen of elms beyond the far wall to filter the southwest wind. Moreover, it was an interesting dogleg shape, a change from the usual rectangle and offering the potential for hidden areas, surprise, and mystery.

A professional and gifted garden designer, Rumary was clear about his aims for this, his own garden. He was determined that materials and style should be in sympathy with the old house, and that there should be a wide-ranging planting plan that could be adapted and increased without detracting from the basic framework of the design. Above all he wanted, in Gertrude Jekyll's words, "to paint a year-long succession of living pictures."

Other requirements were: to reduce traffic noise; to ensure attractive views from the principal windows, with planting to provide year-round interest; to have various areas for sitting and outdoor meals, taking advantage of the sun at different times of day; and to allow room for setting out pots

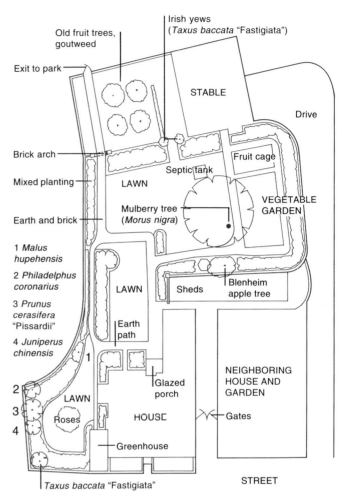

Above The former garden had little cohesion and certainly no overall theme. Mark Rumary saw how its odd corners and features would provide a wonderful opportunity for playing with space and depth.

Left The main lawn and sitting area are framed by the old arch. The success of this garden lies in its separate rooms brought together with a skilled combination of planting.

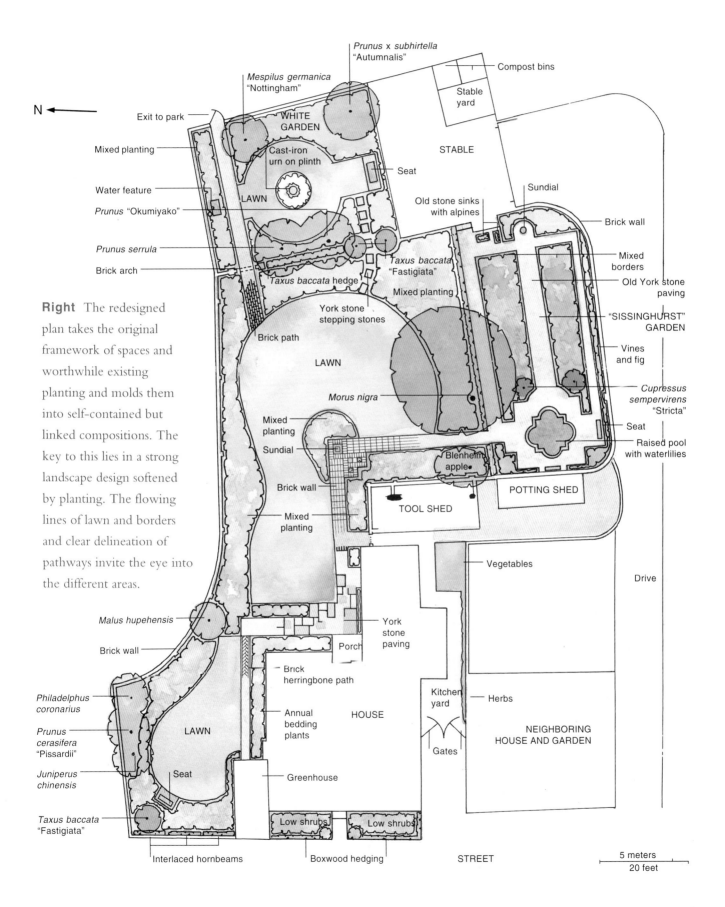

N ◄

Right The redesigned plan takes the original framework of spaces and worthwhile existing planting and molds them into self-contained but linked compositions. The key to this lies in a strong landscape design softened by planting. The flowing lines of lawn and borders and clear delineation of pathways invite the eye into the different areas.

Prunus x subhirtella "Autumnalis"

Mespilus germanica "Nottingham"

Compost bins

Stable yard

STABLE

Exit to park

WHITE GARDEN

Mixed planting

Cast-iron urn on plinth

Seat

Sundial

Water feature

LAWN

Old stone sinks with alpines

Brick wall

Prunus "Okumiyako"

Mixed borders

Prunus serrula

Taxus baccata "Fastigiata"

Old York stone paving

Brick arch

Taxus baccata hedge

Mixed planting

"SISSINGHURST" GARDEN

York stone stepping stones

Vines and fig

Brick path

LAWN

Cupressus sempervirens "Stricta"

Morus nigra

Seat

Mixed planting

Raised pool with waterlilies

Sundial

Blenheim apple

Brick wall

POTTING SHED

Mixed planting

TOOL SHED

Vegetables

Drive

Malus hupehensis

Brick wall

York stone paving

Porch

Brick herringbone path

Kitchen yard

Herbs

Philadelphus coronarius

Annual bedding plants

HOUSE

Prunus cerasifera "Pissardii"

NEIGHBORING HOUSE AND GARDEN

Gates

Juniperus chinensis

LAWN

Seat

Greenhouse

Taxus baccata "Fastigiata"

Low shrubs

Low shrubs

Interlaced hornbeams

Boxwood hedging

STREET

5 meters
20 feet

Right The centrally placed urn in the white garden is planted for summer with *Plectranthus madagascariensis* "Variegated Mintleaf." The bed beneath contains *Begonia* x *carrierei*. Dense evergreen planting obscures the walls.

Opposite Positioned at the point where the path changes direction, the sundial is perfectly placed to lead the eye to the glimpsed church spire – an excellent example of drawing a good view into the composition. Note the *Wisteria sinensis* trained into tree shape.

of half-hardy plants in spring. He also wanted a garden that would be reasonably easy to maintain.

Although the garden is relatively small, about one-third of an acre in all, Rumary saw that an impression of greater space could be achieved by subdividing it into a number of outdoor rooms, each with a self-contained theme held together by skillful plantsmanship. The new design is molded around the original layout, but the latter has been transformed with planting and hedges to form four distinct areas, two of which are formal in character with clearly delineated outlines, and two more relaxed and free-flowing.

There were some difficulties to overcome. Certain areas were shaded for much of the day by overhanging trees and by the high walls, which also created a frost pocket. The sandy soil was poor, and as rainfall here is low the dry shaded areas presented problems. Add to this rampant goutweed, old

diseased fruit trees, and a degenerating network of paths, and it is clear that major restructuring was needed.

The path leading around the side of the house to the stable was rebuilt. It is paved with red brick from the old scullery relieved with blue stable bricks pulled from the former stableyard. Old York stone furnished wider areas of paving.

An old mulberry is the most important of the few trees that were worth keeping, together with a number of Irish yews, a fine philadelphus, and a Chinese juniper. Though the deeds showed that the property had been Magnolia House throughout the nineteenth century, there were no magnolias. Mark included several kinds in his plan, one of the most attractive being *M.* x *loebneri*.

The planting of the garden began with the placing of trees, shrubs, and climbing plants along the walls, using plenty of evergreens. To the south, through the brick arch and

screened by a newly planted yew hedge, is a formal garden largely given over to dark-leaved evergreens, but strongly accented with white-flowered plants, which differ from year to year. White is the only color allowed here, since it stands out particularly well in this shaded area and makes a good contrast to the multicolored remainder of the garden. A small circular lawn surrounds a centrally placed urn, painted white, the focal point of a vista from the terrace. This treatment, with the eye led gently to a framed picture, is reminiscent of Hidcote Manor or Sissinghurst, both in England. This is the "breakfast room" on warm summer mornings, catching the sun early. (The fine backdrop of elms sadly succumbed to disease and was removed, but there is now the advantage of afternoon sun.)

The old mulberry tree is set in a broad area of planting that borders the main lawn, sweeping around the dogleg down toward the house. This planting, kept narrow to leave more room for lawn, draws the two less formal sections of the garden together. This creates a feeling of movement and space – an open glade amidst the dense planting.

A sundial, backed by planting, anchors the right-angle turn of a stretch of brick path, and acts as an important pivotal point. Where the brick path meets the main terrace, the change of use is signaled by a change of material to old York stone. Hard surfaces everywhere are softened by plants.

In the smallest garden room, next to the village street, three hornbeams interlaced above the wall make a high barrier, which has been successful in reducing noise. This space is self-contained, a secret garden where the carefully positioned seat catches a good deal of sun. From here, the longest vista through the main garden is viewed via a tension point: the house framed on one side and the curving brick

wall, clothed in shrubs and vines, on the other.

The old vegetable plot gave way to a formal rectangular framework filled with a cottage-garden-style mixture of plants such as old roses, iris, allium, and ceanothus. It has a romantic air that has won for it the family nickname of "Sissinghurst." A long central axis between overflowing beds is halted by an armillary sphere at one end and a raised, Spanish-courtyard-style pool at the other. The pool sides are just high enough to double as an occasional seat where you can watch fish and enjoy the scent of nearby lilies and the splash of a fountain. Two slender conifers near the pond add a stately touch: they are Italian cypresses raised from seed taken from a tree growing in the local churchyard.

Above A delicious profusion of planting and color in the rectangular garden that fondly recalls Sissinghurst. The pair of Italian cypresses, *Cupressus sempervirens* "Stricta," add to the Mediterranean feel of the raised pool; the rest of the planting has an English cottage-garden feel: *Pyrus salicifolia* "Pendula," *Alstroemeria* Ligtu hybrids, alliums, *Stachys byzantina*, geraniums, *Salvia officinalis* "Purpurascens," romneya, delphiniums, roses, and hollyhocks.

Right Miss Willmott's ghost, *Eryngium giganteum*, placed against the soft leaves of *Senecio cineraria* "White Diamond," makes a lovely foil to the radiant colors in "Sissinghurst."

Right A sheltered, sunny spot in which to relax while enjoying the scent of lilies, a flash of goldfish, and, in late summer, the taste of a warm fig. The stoneware pots contain *Pelargonium* "Frank Headley" and variegated *Felicia amelloides*. On the left, an ornamental grass, *Miscanthus sinensis* "Strictus," towers over the potted lilies.

A musicians' garden

It is hardly surprising that all the gardens I have chosen to feature are outside rooms in the fullest sense, having strong links with the house and suiting the owners in a personal as well as practical way. This garden, designed by Erwan Tymen for two musicians, one of whom is a particularly keen gardener, is much more than an interesting and delightful study in the manipulation of a tiny space.

Erwan Tymen responded imaginatively to his clients' needs: the garden is for them an instrument on which to play, and for which they are constantly composing new themes. Thus he saw his role as consisting essentially of building the basic structures within which a variety of different creative approaches could flourish, according to season or simply whim. To achieve this, he worked closely with his clients at every stage of the garden's development.

The small new town house, in northern France, was built in a corner of the larger garden belonging to the parents of one of the owners. The garden faces south and is almost entirely walled, though retaining access to the parental home. The boundary walls provide seclusion and are plastered white, bringing light to the area and offering a contrast to any planting set against them. A slight change of level has been emphasized with a shallow step to create two distinct spaces. The composition is a balance between the hard landscape structure of the garden and the sculptural use

Opposite Never static, always interesting, the garden reflects its musician owners' current preferences and changing moods. Arranged to resemble musical notation, rails from a brass bedstead introduce a whimsical touch.

Right This composition handles the tiny space with panache. It provides room for sitting, dining, entertaining, and relaxing, within a visually stimulating framework of planting. With space at a premium, and a number of activities to cater for, careful planning is essential. Yet some of the most successful gardens are remarkably small and, like this one, true outdoor rooms.

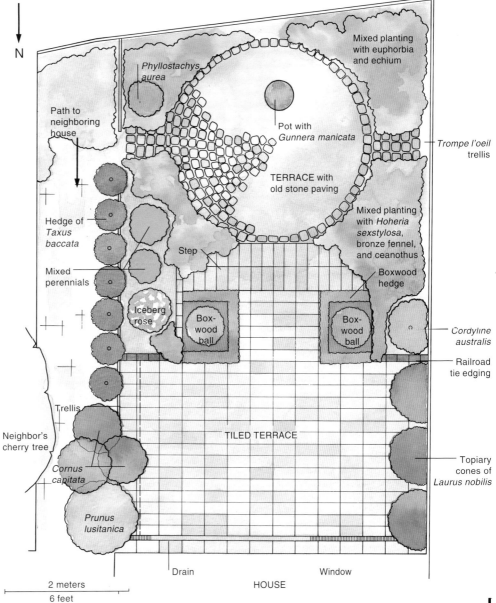

N

Phyllostachys aurea

Path to neighboring house

Mixed planting with euphorbia and echium

Pot with Gunnera manicata

Trompe l'oeil trellis

TERRACE with old stone paving

Hedge of Taxus baccata

Mixed planting with Hoheria sexstylosa, bronze fennel, and ceanothus

Step

Mixed perennials

Boxwood hedge

Iceberg rose

Box-wood ball

Box-wood ball

Cordyline australis

Railroad tie edging

Trellis

TILED TERRACE

Neighbor's cherry tree

Topiary cones of Laurus nobilis

Cornus capitata

Prunus lusitanica

Drain

Window

2 meters

6 feet

HOUSE

of planting that brings both softness and drama.

The terrace next to the house is laid with regular pinkish gray paving that sets off the warm glow of the terra-cotta pots. This area for sitting, dining, and entertaining links naturally with the tiled floor of the interior, through wide glass sliding doors. Trimmed boxwood balls echoed the huge dome of *Argyranthemum frutescens*, which has since been removed, leaving center stage to an Iceberg rose.

The farther terrace is paved in a circular pattern of Belgian blocks. They set up an interesting rhythm around the fine Provençal pot containing the gunnera that holds sway over this area, at the same time diverting attention from the angularity of the boundaries.

Black-stained lumber, an excellent foil for plants, has been extensively used, both for trellising and for deep edging to beds behind low boxwood hedging. Tymen likes the association between wood and metal, the warmth of the one providing a counterpoint to the harshness of the other.

Erwan Tymen insists, and his clients agree, that regular pruning and thinning, particularly of the periphery planting, is essential in order to maintain the balance of different volumes. This clearly makes sense in such a small garden. Planting is the cloak that draws the various elements together, providing color and interest year-round.

Left The gigantic leaves of *Gunnera manicata* grow at a stupendous rate. Here the visual strength of powerful foliage and striking flower heads is counterbalanced by the Provençal pot, intentionally placed off center. It sets up a centrifugal movement – far more interesting than if it were centrally placed. Light and foliage set up their own rhythms, and the more outstanding the foliage, the more important the shadows.

Opposite The invitation to move from indoors to the outdoor room is hard to resist. The squared tiles inside pick up the geometry of the first terrace and clean lines lead the eye to the sculptural leaves of the gunnera, a powerful focal point.

Right Boundaries are softened with planting. A zinc orb, once part of the architectural detailing on an opera house roof, echoes the shape of the boxwood balls and contrasts in texture with the wooden trellis glimpsed on the wall.

Any room, inside or out, will inevitably need a certain amount of maintenance and renewal as wear and tear take their toll. Ongoing outdoor maintenance may entail little more than simply keeping things tidy by sweeping paths or shearing hedges, but from time to time renewal may be needed, perhaps to repair the effects of weather, or in response to changing needs or tastes. A sandbox that was provided for children can become a pool or a flower bed once the children have outgrown its use, a play space can be turned into a vegetable plot. A large expanse of lawn that becomes increasingly difficult to maintain as you grow older might be replanted as an orchard floored with rougher grass, bulbs, and wildflowers.

For efficient garden maintenance and renewal, it is important to have the correct tools and to keep them in peak condition. Good-quality tools may cost more initially, but they provide better service and many will last a lifetime. Be careful to operate all tools safely and to wear protective clothing and headgear when necessary.

While I try to avoid using chemicals, they can be invaluable. Follow instructions to the letter, wear appropriate protective clothing, and store any chemicals in their original packaging in a safe, tamper-proof place and well out of the reach of children.

Stone, brick, concrete, tiles, and gravel
Walls of stone, brick, or concrete have the longest life of any boundary and, if properly constructed, can last hundreds of years. Drystone walls, though, may shift or subside slightly, and some stones, including cope-stones, may need replacing from time to time. Stone or brick walls with mortared joints will need repointing occasionally, especially if a wall is old, in which case it will have been built with soft lime mortar, which erodes more easily. Carry out any repointing very carefully, matching new pointing to old. Be sure to keep the face of the wall clean as you work, and before you rake out the old joints lay a sheet at the bottom of the wall to catch any debris. The raked-out lime and mortar could make a surprising difference to the pH of your soil.

Occasionally the coping on top of a brick wall may deteriorate and individual bricks or the whole run may need taking off and replacing. As with repointing, make sure that any new work matches the old as closely as possible.

Concrete walls rarely need any attention other than replacing damaged coping or renewing cracked rendering.

You can encourage mosses and lichens to grow on drystone walls, or on stone or concrete ornaments, by painting them with milk or yogurt, which speeds colonization. Cow manure is also effective, but it stinks and in hot weather attracts flies. Impatient nonpurists may prefer to use brand name "ageing agents."

The hard surfaces of a garden – paths, paving, steps, ramps, and so on – are subject to a great deal of wear. If paving has been properly laid (see Chapter 4), little or no maintenance is necessary. However, as with walls, should the pointing between the joints in paving deteriorate, you will have to rake it out and renew it.

Old brick or tile paving that is not frost-proof may need attention. Carefully chop out the affected areas and replace them with new frost-proof bricks or tiles, taking care to match the new materials as closely as possible to the old and to lay the new in the same style. This includes taking note of the depth of the old pointing in order to reproduce it, and it may mean rubbing dirt into the new paving to "age" it.

Paving in a shady area may become slippery with age as a result of colonization by algae. Tackle this by washing the paving down, using a stiff broom and soapy water. If this doesn't work, you may need to apply a weak solution of household bleach or a brand name path cleaner, but make sure that you keep any chemicals well away from planted areas.

Provided a gravel path or drive has been properly laid (see Chapter 4), only minimal maintenance should be necessary. Simply check the wooden edge restraints for rot. Gravel, well laid with a binder, should not have a weed growth problem, but if there are weeds, they can easily be controlled with weedkiller.

Wood
Lumber in the garden has a relatively short life, but this can be extended by regular applications of a nontoxic preservative. Fences, doors, arches, pergolas, or arbors in exposed conditions will need an annual application; in sheltered areas, an application every three years is usually enough. Before applying the preservative, carefully take down any vines – a task that is easier if they have been trained on wires. Take this opportunity to check the condition of the wires and to replace them if necessary. They can easily be repositioned once the preservative has dried.

It is difficult to apply preservative to wooden trellis, because it is usually covered with vines. This makes it all the more important to check regularly for rot and renew as necessary.

Provided they are well built, pergolas rarely rot, except perhaps at the base of the posts; check here carefully and renew any decayed lumber.

Slatted fences can be kept in good condition by renewing individual slats and replacing gravel boards from time to time. With fences made of interwoven panels or wattle hurdles, complete panels may have to be renewed. At the same time, check the supporting posts for rot and renew them if necessary. Painted fences and doors should be checked for wear and tear and repainted whenever necessary.

Wooden decks, steps, and ramps need attention too, but replacing any damaged or rotted areas should be fairly straightforward. When you undertake the original construction, keep a number of spare boards and store them outside. These can be used for repair work and will be a better color match than new lumber. As with fences, make a regular application of a nontoxic wood preservative every one to three years, depending on exposure. Check vulnerable areas such as main bearers and posts, steps, and handrails; also use a nail punch to drive home any nails that have pushed themselves through the surface.

Always keep the space beneath decks, steps, or ramps clear to assist air circulation.

Resist the temptation to use this area for storage, as without free circulation of air the wood will rot. To prevent accidents on surfaces that may have become slippery, scrub them over with a weak solution of household bleach. Check the lumber of gazebos and summerhouses regularly and apply preservative or paint when necessary. While you are checking the lumber, also remember to look at the roof, replace any broken windowpanes, and clear the gutters of fallen leaves and other debris.

All furniture is probably best kept under cover in winter. Wooden furniture should be treated every winter with an appropriate oil such as boiled linseed oil, or (for teak and certain hardwoods) teak oil.

Metal
Metal railings, gates, arches, and garden furniture should be checked annually for rust. Rub down and repaint if necessary.

Lighting
Properly installed lighting should not need any maintenance, apart from cleaning and changing bulbs. Check any visible wiring to make sure it is securely connected and the insulation is intact, but for safety's sake always employ a licensed electrician for any repairs or renewal.

Water
To minimize pool maintenance, try to locate pools in the open, where there will be little leaf fall into the water. You should also buy your plants from a good aquatic center where you will get sound advice on what is suitable for your particular pool. For instance, if you have a small pond you need to be sure that the plants you buy are not going to prove too vigorous. As a general rule any cleaning out of pools is to be avoided as far as possible, because cleaning can disrupt the ecosystem. Any excessive buildup of leaves and mud can be removed, but you should always leave some, as it is an important part of the pond-life habitat. Sometimes, when you have a large fish population, toxins can build up. In this case, in late autumn, empty out about a quarter of the water and refill with fresh.

It is important to ensure that a pond does not freeze over entirely in cold weather. Aquatic centers supply various devices to prevent freezing. Where prolonged thick ice is expected, an immersion heater can be installed to keep an area open; and a black float placed on the surface will absorb sunlight and melt a hole in thin ice. But, except in very cold climates, it is usually quite sufficient just to gently break a hole in the ice. What you must never do is hit the ice hard, as the shock may stun the fish.

If you have a pump, check and clean the filter from time to time to make sure the jets are clear.

Trees
The first essential, of course, is to choose the right tree for the right spot: the folly of planting a weeping willow in a small front garden is obvious. A tree which needs ample space, planted in a confined area, can only be kept under control by constant hacking; the result will be a misshapen and decidedly unhappy specimen.

Always prepare the ground well for planting, with good topsoil, some planting compost, and an application of slow-release fertilizer. Stake the sapling well and secure it with tree ties, which should be checked regularly and slackened as the tree grows.

If tree surgery is needed to thin the crown or reduce the height of a mature tree, employ the services of a qualified arborist. Tree work is highly skilled and in the wrong hands can be dangerous.

Shrubs: pruning
The objectives of pruning a shrub are to remove dead, diseased, or weak wood, to encourage healthy growth, to maintain a good shape, and to promote flowering.

This book does not pretend to be a pruning manual, and you are advised to buy a good book on the subject. However, there are a few general guidelines that can usefully be given here.

Any pruning cut should be made at a sloping angle, just above a bud. The bottom of the cut should be level with the bud, on the opposite side of the stem.

As a general rule, shrubs that flower early in the year, on the previous year's growth, should be pruned immediately after flowering, to allow the new flowering stems to grow for the following season. Those that flower later in the year, on the current year's growth, need attention in early spring.

There are also plants, including several dogwoods and smaller ornamental willows, that are grown for the bright color of their young stems in winter. Cut these to within 18in/450mm of the ground in early spring to produce bright new growth for the coming winter.

Rose pruning is a complex subject, but as a general rule the wild species and their hybrids, including shrub roses, need light pruning; Hybrid Tea roses and Floribundas, on the other hand, are usually pruned more severely. Climbing roses are an exception: regardless of group they need little pruning apart from the removal of weak or diseased stems.

Hedges
Regular trimming is essential to keep a hedge under control. The frequency with which you have to shear depends on the species (see pp.79-80). All hedges benefit from being sheared into a wedge shape, with the top slightly narrower than the bottom. This allows ample light and air to penetrate down to ground level.

To bring a neglected or overgrown hedge under control, cut it hard back over two or three years and fertilize it regularly. Provided the hedge is not very old, cutting back will improve its growth and speed maturity.

Hardy perennials
Most hardy perennials that die down each winter and reappear the following spring tend to become less vigorous as they get old. Every three years or so, in early spring just before growth starts, lift the plants, cut away the central area, and then divide and replant the healthy outer sections. As well as being beneficial to the plants, this is an excellent way to increase your stock and create additional swaths of planting.

Lawns and ground-cover plants
Lawns and ground-cover plants call for regular attention if they are to look their best. All types of grass should be fertilized in spring, summer, and autumn. Spring is the time to weed them, to scarify to remove accumulated debris, and to spike them to aerate the surface and promote healthy root growth. Mow your lawn regularly during the growing season, using a mower with sharp blades, but be sure not to cut the

grass too short. Cutting it any shorter than ½in/10mm weakens it, leaving it open to dieback in hot, dry weather, as well as to competition from weeds and moss.

Ground-cover plants, too, benefit from a regular fertilizing with a liquid fertilizer. Some ground-cover plants are invasive, which is fine where you want to cover an area completely, but where you have more delicate plants that might be overrun, check the growth of the ground cover regularly and either cut it back or dig out those areas that might become a problem.

Fertilizing

Oddly enough, most people remember to fertilize small decorative plants, but bigger ones, such as trees, hedges, and large shrubs, often tend to get forgotten. The addition of nutrients, particularly at the time of planting and in the early stages of a plant's development, can make a very considerable difference to its subsequent growth. And an ongoing program of fertilizing is essential to maintain a healthy garden.

Watering

The other vital ingredient, apart from food, is water. In many parts of the world, even in temperate climates, rainfall is irregular and additional watering may be necessary. Take care, however, not to overirrigate, because a plant that does not have to reach down into the soil for water will never develop a vigorous root system, and so will be generally weaker, and susceptible to drought. It is most important that irrigation should be economical, and that it should get the water to where it is needed.

Irrigation methods can range from the simplest of hand-held watering cans to a fully computerized system that can be programmed to operate at specific times of day and under predetermined conditions. Such a computerized system can include "pop-up" heads for lawns and drip-feed pipes for borders. Some systems, hand-held or automatic, also allow fertilizers to be incorporated into a water line.

It is always sensible to have one or more supply faucets fitted in distant parts of the garden. If possible, you should also have a couple of barrels to collect rainwater. Being free of lime, rainwater is invaluable for watering calcifuge plants; and a water barrel can be a lifesaver in times of drought.

BIBLIOGRAPHY

Balston, Michael *The Well-Furnished Garden* Mitchell Beazley, London 1986

The Bauhaus – Masters and Students by Themselves Conran Octopus, London 1992

Beazley, Elizabeth *Design and Detail of the Space Between Buildings* Architectural Press, London 1968

Brookes, John *Room Outside* Thames and Hudson, London 1968

Brown, Jane *The Art and Architecture of English Gardens* Weidenfeld and Nicolson, London 1989

Church, Thomas D. *Your Private World* Chronicle Books, San Francisco 1983

— *Gardens Are for People* McGraw Hill, New York 1983

Eckbo, Garrett *The Art of Home Landscape* McGraw Hill, New York 1956

— *Philosophy of Landscape* Process Architecture Publishing Co, Tokyo 1990

Ferguson, Nichola *Right Plant Right Place* Pan, London 1986

Frankel, Felice and Johnson, Jory *Modern Landscape Architecture* Abbeville Press, New York 1991

Halprin, Lawrence *Changing Places* San Francisco Museum of Modern Art, San Francisco 1986

Iglauer, Edith *Seven Stones: A Portrait of Arthur Erickson* Harbor Publishing, University of Washington Press, Seattle 1981

Innes, Jocasta *Exterior Detail* Collins and Brown, London 1990

Itoh, Teiji *The Gardens of Japan* Kodansha International Ltd, New York 1989

Lloyd Wright, Frank *Maste Drawings from the Frank Lloyd Wright Archives* Thames and Hudson, London 1990

Lyall, Sutherland *Designing the New Landscape* Thames and Hudson, London 1991

Lutyens, Edwin *Architectural Monographs 6* Academy Editions, London/New York 1986

Oehme, Wolfgang and Van Sweden, James *Bold Romantic Gardens* Acropolis Books, Virginia 1990

Sunset New Western Garden Book Lane Publishing Co, Menlo Park, California 1979

Tunnard, Christopher *Gardens in the Modern Landscape* Architectural Press, London 1950

Walker, Peter *Landscape as Art* Process Architecture Publishing Co, Tokyo 1989

INDEX

ACKNOWLEDGMENTS

Author's Acknowledgments

Although the author has his name on the front of a book, he is only the tip of an iceberg.

I should like to thank everyone at Frances Lincoln for their support, hard work and never-failing enthusiasm.

A special thanks to Anne Kilborn, who is quite the best editor I have worked with, for her patience, good humour and complete lack of panic even under the greatest pressure.

Niki Medlikova designed this book and it can be difficult for two designers to work together. However, the end result is terrific and we quickly became firm friends – thanks Niki.

Thanks to my old friend Jerry Harpur for the superb worldwide photography and invaluable contacts with farflung clients.

Finally, thank you to all the inspirational designers whose work forms a great part of this book. Studying their techniques and excellence has taken my own work a step forward.

Publishers' Acknowledgments

We thank the following people for allowing us to photograph their gardens, Susan Gernaey, Ray and Anita Green, Howard and Tina Reuben, Tracey Rose, Diana Ross; Ann Alexander-Sinclair for allowing us to photograph the author in her garden.

We are particularly grateful to all the owners and designers (unless otherwise specified one person embodied both roles) who gave so generously of their time in providing information about the 'outdoor rooms' featured in Chapter 6: Julian and Helene Elliott (pp.144-7); Yvon-Serge Lesné and designer Timothy Vaughan (pp.148-51); Ruth Borun and designer Chris Rosmini (pp.152-7); designer Jacques Wirtz (pp.158-61); Christopher Masson (pp.162-5); Landscape Architects Wolfgang Oehme and James Anthony van Sweden (pp.166-9); Mrs Bernard Riley (pp.170-3); Mark Rumary (pp.174-9); Messieurs Montfort and Merson and designer Erwan Tymen (pp.180-3).

Thanks to Jerry Harpur for putting his splendid pictures in context and for his research on featured gardens.

We thank the following people for their help in producing this book: Joanna Chisholm, Jo Christian, Sally Cracknell, Sue Gladstone, Hilary Hockman, John Laing, Diana Loxley, Sarah Mitchell, Annabel Morgan, Sara Robin and Louise Tucker.

Line artwork *Joseph Kent* and *Oxford Illustrators Limited*
Watercolour illustrations *Sally Launder*

Photographic Acknowledgments

a=above b=below l=left r=right m=middle d=designer

Geoff Dann 42m ©FLL; Garden Picture Library/Gary Rogers 85 John Glover 142,143; Jerry Harpur 1, 2, 5, 6, 7, 8, 9, 10, 11, 14 (Sandra Ovenstone, Capetown), 16 (d: Christopher Masson), 17 (d: Chris Rosmini), 18, 19 (Gwladys Tongue, Bucks), 21, 22, 23 (Lower Hall, Shropshire), 26/27, 29, 30 (Sandra Ovenstone, Capetown, d: David Hicks), 31, 32, 33 (d: Gary van Egmond), 34a, 35 (Dot Presbury, Johannesburg), 40/41, 42a (d: Berry's Garden Co), 42b (Barnsley House, Gloucestershire), 44, 45 (Hazelbury Manor, Wiltshire), 46, 47, 50, 51, 52 (John Bodie, Coombelands, Sussex), 53, 54, 55, 56, 57 (d: Gunilla Pickard), 60l (Cranborne Manor, Hampshire), 60r, 61l, 62/63 (Seattle), 64, 66a (Liz Longhurst, Sydney), 66b (Hazelbury Manor, Wiltshire), 67, 68l (Bramdean House, Hampshire), 68r, 69l (Mrs Kettley, Natal), 69r, 70, 71, 72, 73, 74, 75, 77, 78a (d: Michael Balston), 78b, 80 (Mr and Mrs Malcolm Skinner, Eastgrove Cottage, Hereford and Worcester), 81 (Seattle), 82a, 82bl (d: Mark Rumary), 82br and 83a (d: Martin Lane Fox), 83bl (John Bodie, Coombelands, Sussex), 83br (d: Bruce Kelly), 84 (Manor Farm, Somerset), 87, 89, 90a, 91a, 91b (Panmure, South Australia), 92, 93l (Park Farm, Essex), 93r, 94b, 95b, 96, 97, 98l, 99,100b, 101, 102, 103, 105, 106a (Bobbi Hicks, Sydney), 106b (Frances Denby, 'Dolwen', North Wales), 107a, 107b (Sandra Ovenstone, Capetown), 110/ 111, 114, 115 (Park Farm, Essex), 117, 118 (Lady Barbirolli, London), 119a, 119m (Burford House, Shropshire), 119bl, 119br, 121l, 122r, 125r (John Burgee, New York), 126l, 126r (Sally Masson, New Zealand), 127a, 128, 129, 130, 131, 132, 133, 134, 135l (Lower Hall, Shropshire), 135r, 136, 137 (Sara Robinson, London), 138/139, 145, 146, 147, 152, 154, 155, 156, 157, 163, 164, 165, 170, 172, 173, 174, 176, 177, 178, 179; Jacqui Hurst 122l ©FLL (John Hilton, London), Peter C Jones/Liaison International 12/13, 61r, 86b, 94a, 98r, 125l; Michèle Lamontagne 28, 65; Andrew Lawson 90b; Leisuredeck Ltd 100a; Georges Lévêque 124, 149, 150, 151, 158, 160, 161, 180, 182, 183; John Neubauer 48, 49, 166, 168, 169; Clive Nichols 59 ©FLL, 76, 86a (Mr & Mrs D Terry, Hereford and Worcester), 95a ©FLL, 113, 121r ©FLL, 123 ©FLL, 127b ©FLL (d: Sue Gernaey); Gary Rogers 34b, 88, 104; Steve Wooster 58, 112

Editor *Anne Kilborn*
Art Editor *Niki Medlikova*
Indexer *Kathy Gill*
Page make-up *Jon Anderson*
Horticultural Consultant *Tony Lord*

Editorial Director *Erica Hunningher*
Art Director *Caroline Hillier*
Picture Editor *Anne Fraser*
Production *Annemarieke Kroon*